THE LAYMAN'S BIBLE COMMENTARY

THE LAYMAN'S BIBLE COMMENTARY
IN TWENTY-FIVE VOLUMES

THE LAYMAN'S
BIBLE COMMENTARY

Balmer H. Kelly, *Editor*

Donald G. Miller   *Associate Editors*   Arnold B. Rhodes

Dwight M. Chalmers, *Editor, John Knox Press*

VOLUME 21

THE LETTER OF PAUL TO THE

ROMANS

THE FIRST LETTER OF PAUL TO THE

CORINTHIANS

THE SECOND LETTER OF PAUL TO THE

CORINTHIANS

Kenneth J. Foreman

JOHN KNOX PRESS

Atlanta

Published in Great Britain by SCM Press Ltd., London.

Eighth printing 1976

Complete set: ISBN: 0-8042-3026-9
This volume: 0-8042-3021-8
Library of Congress Card Number: 59-10454
Printed in the United States of America

PREFACE

The LAYMAN'S BIBLE COMMENTARY is based on the conviction that the Bible has the Word of good news for the whole world. The Bible is not the property of a special group. It is not even the property and concern of the Church alone. It is given to the Church for its own life but also to bring God's offer of life to all mankind —wherever there are ears to hear and hearts to respond.

It is this point of view which binds the separate parts of the LAYMAN'S BIBLE COMMENTARY into a unity. There are many volumes and many writers, coming from varied backgrounds, as is the case with the Bible itself. But also as with the Bible there is a unity of purpose and of faith. The purpose is to clarify the situations and language of the Bible that it may be more and more fully understood. The faith is that in the Bible there is essentially one Word, one message of salvation, one gospel.

The LAYMAN'S BIBLE COMMENTARY is designed to be a concise non-technical guide for the layman in personal study of his own Bible. Therefore, no biblical text is printed along with the comment upon it. This commentary will have done its work precisely to the degree in which it moves its readers to take up the Bible for themselves.

The writers have used the Revised Standard Version of the Bible as their basic text. Occasionally they have differed from this translation. Where this is the case they have given their reasons. In the main, no attempt has been made either to justify the wording of the Revised Standard Version or to compare it with other translations.

The objective in this commentary is to provide the most helpful explanation of fundamental matters in simple, up-to-date terms. Exhaustive treatment of subjects has not been undertaken.

In our age knowledge of the Bible is perilously low. At the same time there are signs that many people are longing for help in getting such knowledge. Knowledge of and about the Bible is, of course, not enough. The grace of God and the work of the Holy Spirit are essential to the renewal of life through the Scriptures. It is in the happy confidence that the great hunger for the Word is a sign of God's grace already operating within men, and that the Spirit works most wonderfully where the Word is familiarly known, that this commentary has been written and published.

THE EDITORS AND
THE PUBLISHERS

THE LETTER OF PAUL TO THE

ROMANS

INTRODUCTION

A Personal Note to the Reader

Who are you? I wish I knew. The list of writers which you will find on this volume tells you who I am, but who are you? You are a "layman"—but that means simply a person without technical training and special knowledge in this particular field. You have never had seminary training. You are probably not able to read the New Testament in the Greek language in which it was written. You have never done any graduate study in the field of the Bible or religion. Beyond that, you may be almost anybody except a very young teen-ager or a child. You may be a graduate of high school or of college, or even of a graduate school with an M.D. or a Ph.D. to your credit. In any case, you are an interested person or you would not be reading this.

This may be the first commentary on the Bible you ever read. Don't let that bother you. This is the first one I ever wrote. Some of the greatest saints and most brilliant scholars in the Christian world, past and present, have written better commentaries on Romans than this one is going to be. But let us not part company for that. Just because this commentary was not written by one of the great minds, you can have the consolation of knowing that if I can understand Romans you can understand it. And after all, writing a commentary on a book whose author is dead and gone is a risky business. Over and over again we shall wish we had the author right here for an interview. But that is out of bounds.

One thing is certain: if you are seriously interested in the kind of thing that interested the man who wrote Romans (and this holds good for books outside the Bible, too), then you will seriously try to find out what he said and what he meant. And we shall be finding out, all the way along, that the problems which were of burning interest to Paul are not, in our day, mere buckets of ashes.

Why a Commentary?

Why do you want a commentary at all? You do not ask for one in order to read the morning paper or a letter. Why do you need one for the Bible? What is there about Romans, for example, that makes it harder to understand than the morning paper or a letter from a friend?

For one thing, the Letter to the Romans now on your desk is not written in the kind of English a newspaper reporter or your writing friend would use. When the Roman Christians read it or heard it read, they found it to be in precisely the ordinary everyday Greek that everyone spoke. But the kind of English used in our standard Bibles today is a kind seldom spoken any more outside of Church or poetry.

This difficulty can be cleared up by reading Romans in one of the unofficial fresh translations of Paul's Greek into the language we actually use when writing simple English prose today. Every present-day translation may be in itself a valuable commentary.

But the difficulties are not over when you get the letter into modern English. For this letter was not written yesterday, but nineteen centuries ago. It was not written in any existing nation, but in the Roman Empire. Customs, habits, traditions, business, recreation, culture, art, government—everything was different then. Any kind of writing "reflects the culture" of the times and the place where it was written. To take one single example: in Paul's day slavery was a universally accepted fact. Today we regard slavery, wherever it still exists, as barbaric and unchristian. It was an age that had not known Christianity. Ours is an age that has been familiar with Christianity for centuries. Then, society had never been affected by Christian or Jewish ideals. Today, over much of the world, Christian ideals are taken for granted even by persons who are not Christians.

Then the Church itself was quite different, as we shall see. Not one of the usual features of the Church of today was then in existence. The church at Rome, for instance, had no official creed, no resident pastor, no Sunday school, no special place of meeting, no order of service, no "program." Any of us would find such a church strange if we walked into it. And naturally we feel a certain strangeness about a letter written to it.

There are also difficulties in ancient letters like these of Paul's which are caused by peculiar varieties of thought and of style. Some sentences are very long and complicated. Since Paul dictated most of his letters, one may suspect that some of the difficulties the modern reader has in reading them come from the fact that Paul talked too fast for his secretary.

One more bar to easy understanding of letters which at their first reading were far easier than now is the fact that the reader unfamiliar with them may not know just who wrote them, or to whom they were written, or what circumstances called for each letter. When you open your friend's letter you know who he is, you have known him for years, you know how he expresses himself, you can read his mind. But a letter nearly two thousand years old is another matter. When you open your newspaper you know the background, you have been keeping up with what is going on around the world and in your own home and country. But when you open this ancient letter you do not have the same "feel" for ancient Rome or Corinth—lost cities now—that you do for New York, London, or Homeville.

With all such difficulties a commentary is expected to be helpful. But no number of commentaries can be any substitute for personal digging in the Bible by yourself. The great essentials stand out in the Bible plainly enough.

Author

Who wrote Romans? The Apostle Paul, beyond a doubt. There are books in the Bible whose traditional authors are certainly not the real authors. There are other books whose authorship has been questioned but which were probably written by their traditional authors. Still other books have never had their authorship seriously questioned. Romans is one of these. Keep this in mind as we study it. Here is a firsthand document *right out of the generation that could remember Jesus of Nazareth,* a first-class witness to Christian life, problems, and thought in those early years.

Paul is so well known that we need not tell his story here. The Book of Acts and his own letters, which make up a quarter of the New Testament, give us more personal information about him than we have about most figures of ancient history. What we need to bear in mind, reading Romans, is that at the time Paul wrote this letter he was a man in middle life, a man of profound and lasting enthusiasms. He was not a man content to believe and keep silence. He wanted others to believe as he did. Before he became a Christian, he was very fierce against his opponents. They did not have to be opponents; all they had to do to earn his hatred was to believe differently, and he would persecute them to the death when he could. As a Christian he had learned that torture and murder are not weapons of God's truth, but he still drew very sharp lines and never left doubt about where he stood. By the time he wrote Romans he had become a well-known, perhaps the best-known, missionary to non-Jews, a leader in the Church.

At the time this letter was written, Paul had never been in Rome. Many Bible students think that chapter 16 did not originally belong with Romans but is a misplaced sheet of a letter to Ephesus. (More about this when we come to it.) In any case he no doubt knew people in Rome as you know people in some large faraway city. But one great difference between Romans and the Corinthian Letters is that Romans was written to a strange church, while First and Second Corinthians were written to one of the churches Paul knew best, one he had started himself. This gives Corinthians a friendly, familiar tone, and keeps Romans courteous but a bit on the stiff side.

Recipients

What kind of church was at Rome? Neither Paul nor Peter had been there at this time. Traveling Christians from different parts of the Empire, mostly from the eastern end of the Mediterranean, had come to Rome, had made contact with one another, and were (as we would think) an unorganized but going religious community. They were not monks or nuns; they were not professional religious people. There were no "ordained" leaders by any title. It was a church without a whole Bible. The Jewish members, to be sure, had the Hebrew Scriptures, which they brought with them from the Synagogue when they became Christians, but probably few would have owned a complete copy. There was no New Testament in existence. Our four Gospels had not yet been written. Paul had written a few letters, but no one at that time labeled them "Bible"; not even Paul himself thought of them as "Scripture."

So this Letter to the Romans would be the first piece of strictly Christian literature the Roman Christians had ever seen. Paul knew this and so took considerable pains with the letter. (Tradition says he sent a copy of it to a church which he knew very well, the church at Ephesus.) This was to be a kind of handbook on Christian faith and life, a handbook all could use.

Paul was aware, of course, that the Christian church at Rome would turn out to be an extremely important one. As a Roman citizen and proud of it, he well knew the influence of a church in the capital city of an empire. He knew that if that church took his letter seriously and studied it and used it, its influence would carry great weight in many places. So he took his time and wrote more pages to these unknown Romans than to any other church at one time.

Purpose

Why did Paul write this letter? Why he wrote it to the Romans we have just seen. But why did he write it at all? Here we note another difference between Romans and Corinthians. The Corinthian Letters were written to deal with problems in the church at Corinth, problems about which members of that church had told him. But Paul had not started the Roman church, and had had no letter from Rome. He could well claim to be a pastor of the Corinthian church; but to the Romans he was a distinguished "guest minister" by mail, nothing more.

But if Paul does not speak to the problems of the Roman church as such, he does have some pressing problems in mind, and deals with them with a kind of vigorous sublimity. There were three of these in particular that bothered Paul. They were, in fact, nothing less than perverted, distorted varieties of Christianity, or substitutes for it. Paul had run into them where he had been, and knew they would make their way to Rome sooner or later. If these versions of Christianity, which he recognized as perversions, ever won the mind of the whole Church, Paul knew that would be the end of the true faith. As we go through the letter we shall see how he dealt with these. For the present we shall make a short explanation of each one.

The Judaizers' "Christianity"

When we refer to the Judaizers' "Christianity" we use this word because it is familiar, though it had not come into use in Paul's time. The Judaizers had hounded Paul all over the place.

They had tried in the first place to beat him down at a council of
Apostles and other leaders at Jerusalem a few years before this;
but the council voted to support Paul. This did not shut off the
Judaizers. Wherever he went, they followed. They insisted that
his converts were not true Christians. A true Christian, they said,
is one who keeps the laws God has set down in his Holy Scripture. All the promises of God in Scripture are made to Jews, and
so if one wants to be a Christian, the only way leads through
Judaism. (That, of course, is why they were called Judaizers.)
What the Judaizers wanted, in effect, was to make the Christian
faith a sect of Judaism. If they had succeeded, Christianity today
would be—like Sadduceeism, for example—something dead and
gone, to be looked up in an encyclopedia.

The Moralizers' "Christianity"

Paul never mentions the Judaizers or this second group by
name. But the problem they pose is always in his mind. The
"moralizers"—to give them a name—were people who were
about to turn Christianity into a set of rules and regulations. In
our own time a French sociologist has defined religion as a "set of
scruples." That means, a set of "don'ts," "mustn'ts," "shouldn'ts,"
and "can'ts." That is just what Christianity would turn into if the
moralizers had their way. It would end by being a prison for the
free.

Furthermore, the moralizers (and their spiritual successors today) added another feature: by carefully doing this and not doing that, by keeping the rules and never getting demerits, one
earns the favor of God, who gives a man heaven on the strength
of his moral report card. On this view, God's love and grace have
a price, and the price is good behavior. One exchanges a mere
seventy years of good (well, moderately good) behavior for an
eternity of bliss. What a bargain! It sounds simple, too. So Paul
has to explain very clearly that God's favor cannot be bought.
It is not for sale, and no man would have the price of it if it
were.

Anti-law "Christianity"

"Anti-law Christianity" (a long word for it is "Antinomian-
ism") is opposed to law—not as a criminal is opposed to it, but
opposed to the whole idea of having law at all. The common
criminal is just against laws; the anti-law Christian thinks he

doesn't need any. The anti-law Christian is the opposite of the moralizer. He knows that he cannot reach God by any ladder of good deeds, so he concludes that the Ten Commandments all went out when Jesus came, and love has now taken their place. He will say that if one's heart is right he may do as he pleases; love covers a multitude of sins, and so on. Christianity, however, would eventually run down, rot, and be rejected by decent people if this notion were generally adopted.

Not all the problems and ideas we encounter on the pages of Romans fit under these three heads. We shall pick up others in plenty as we go on. But these are in the background of most of what Paul has to say.

Yet to speak of this letter as if it were all "problems and ideas" is to misrepresent it. That, in fact, is what too often has been done to it. It has been made a kind of happy hunting ground for theologies. But in fact, the main and central interest of Romans is, in one word, *life*—life in Christ, life for Christ. The letter comes out of Paul's genuine, life-changing experience, yet it points not to Paul but to his Lord. Jesus Christ is the center of this book. As Paul lets us see him from first one angle and then another, we begin to realize that there is more to Christianity than we had supposed. The conventional, the churchly, the "pious," vanish like plastic at the touch of a hot bulb; as a present-day translator of the New Testament says, working through the New Testament is like installing electricity in an old house and suddenly coming on a live wire. Wherever men have rediscovered the living light to which this old yet new letter is a witness, life itself has become new.

Origin and Place in the Canon

Where and when was Romans written? For good reasons, which may be found in a Bible dictionary, historians are generally agreed that Romans was written from the city of Corinth, at the time Paul spent three months there just after he had been working in Ephesus for more than two years. This was in the winter or early spring of the year A.D. 57-58—only twenty-five years or so after the Resurrection. When Paul talks of the Crucifixion and the Resurrection, he talks of events within the memory of a great many people by no means old. (This date of A.D. 57-58 may be off by two or three years.)

How did Romans come to be a part of the Bible? It came about in the simplest possible way. People who read it, or had it read to them (for many Christians were illiterate), were struck by it. Its truth and force spoke for it convincingly. In short, the Church took this letter to its heart and treasured it. Precisely how it become known in the churches outside of Rome we do not know. There are two ideas on this. The older one is that this letter, like all the others we have from Paul, was hailed as new Bible, so to speak, from the first day it was received and opened. The church receiving it would make copies and circulate them, and other churches—Corinth among them—would do the same with their letters. Another view, newer and gaining supporters, is that the letters of Paul, while welcomed at the time in the various churches, were gradually neglected and forgotten for some thirty years or so. Then the Book of Acts came out, a book of which Paul (humanly speaking) is the principal hero. Under that stimulus, some person or persons collected all the writings of Paul that could then be found and published them, as we would say, in one volume. This proposition has one solid piece of evidence in its favor: none of the writings of the New Testament which can be dated before about A.D. 90 shows an acquaintance with Paul's letters; but every book of the New Testament which can be dated after about A.D. 90 or 95 shows that the writer knew Paul's letters. This would indicate, some people believe, that many if not all the letters of Paul were published about A.D. 90 in one group.

The Thought of Romans

The following is an attempt to follow the thought of the letter, avoiding formal and traditional language so far as possible. A more formal outline will come later. In this summary, descriptive headings have been used as an aid to understanding.

Personal Preface (1:1-15)

Dear Unknown Friends:

Since you have never seen me, let me give you a few words on who I am and why I am writing to you. My name is Paul; my business that of a man whom God has set apart to be a witness to the good news about God. This good news concerns Christ, the

Son of God and our supreme Authority. I am, so to speak, his ambassador to all nations, including yourselves, for you too have been called by God to belong to Jesus Christ. I pray God's blessing on every one of you.

I thank God for you, because the whole world knows of your faith. I have been praying for you; I am anxious to see you. It will do me good to see you, and I hope I can do *you* good. In fact, I have often intended to visit you but I never could. I am eager to announce the good news to you Romans.

Main Theme and Keynote (1:16-17)

This good news is something I am humbly proud to bring to every man who will open his mind and heart to it—and I mean everybody, whether Jews or Gentiles. This good news is nothing less than God's making clear to us what had never been clear before, namely, how he has made it possible for men to live with him unashamed and unafraid—how it is possible for God to look on us with approval. The good news is really the secret that all religions have sought and missed—even I myself for years; in a word, what God's gift is to men of faith, and what the life of faith, beginning with faith and growing toward a more perfect faith, can be.

How the Human Race Has Run to Ruin (1:18—3:20)

The great problem of mankind in general, and of each person in particular, is how to be rightly related to God. If God is against us, we are lost. If God is for us, we don't care what or who may be against us. But how can God be for us? He is free from the least stain of evil, and we human beings are full of evil; we are rotting with it. All I have to do is walk down the street in Corinth and see sickening evidence of the horrible mess man has made of his own life.

It is not just the notorious criminals who are against God and prefer their own ways to his. The nice people, the best people, the religious people, even religious professionals such as I have been—we are all tarred with the same brush. We are infected with the same disease, and the name of it is "sin." Sin is the name for our running away from God, for our making little tin gods out of our own sleazy selves. Even in the act of despising the criminal classes we show ourselves up for conceited hypocrites.

The holy God cannot possibly be friendly to this sort of thing.

He does not need to send people to hell; all he needs to do is
just give people up to their own ways, to let them live in the hell
they have made for themselves.

Religions all are concerned with this problem, but they have
never solved it. The best religion to date, the Jewish, has really
got no further than building a ladder to heaven out of "good
deeds," that is to say, keeping the Law. But a man can keep the
Law very well—I myself have a clean conscience on that score—
and yet not really be in harmony with God after all.

All men are sinners—which is another way of saying all men
have missed the road to God. Some men aren't interested in finding that road; they would rather pray to a cow, or a ghost, than
to God. Others build their own roads, but they go nowhere. One
kind of sinner openly despises God, and another kind of sinner
despises God in another way, namely, by thinking God's good
favor has a price mark on it, that it can be earned or paid for by
something one does.

It won't work. The whole world is accountable to God, the
whole world stands at the bar of his court, before a Judge from
whom there is no appeal; and his verdict is "Guilty."

How God's Prisoner Under Sentence Can Be Set Free (3:21—4:25)

But are there no good people in the world, you will ask. Certainly—as compared with bad people. But the real standard of
good is not man but God. You can define sin as coming short
of the glory of God. I mean failing to have, and to show, those
Godlike qualities that you would expect from those who are made
"in the image of God." He made us to be like himself, and when we
are not, that is sin. Once admit that, and you have to admit that
all men have sinned, for where will you find a man who measures up to the "glory of God"? Furthermore, who can *earn* the
good will, the grace, of God?

Man is in a hopeless case. But God himself has come to man's
rescue. Here is the good news: *God's grace is a gift, and it comes
to us in Jesus.* If we think of God as standing above an altar,
Christ is the sacrifice on that altar. If we think of God on the
judge's bench, Christ takes the place of the condemned man.
What Christ was and did and suffered was for us. Calvary, the
death of Christ, is the strange open door to God.

For everyone? Yes, for all who will. But some will not. The
grace of God, as Christ makes it real for us and in us, is only

for those who humbly and simply take it. There is a name for this simple thing, for just accepting God's gift: the name is *faith*. Faith is not struggling to come closer to God. Faith is not just another step carved out for the climb up God's holy mountain. You can't do it that way. Faith is just opening your heart and letting God give you—himself.

Abraham is the perfect example of what I am talking about. He believed God. It was as simple as that. He trusted God, he obeyed God, he left his life in God's care. This is faith, just taking joyfully what God gives.

Results and Reflections on the Life of God's Children (5:1—8:39)

I would not try to put into one figure of speech all that is true about the new relationship between God and man when we turn to him in faith. The life of faith is not merely believing something we did not believe before. It is not anything added to life; it is new life itself, a new kind of' life. It is as if we lived in a new world—of peace after wartime, hope after despair—in a life which has no darkness, because it is filled with the light of God's love. It is being reconciled to a former enemy.

It is like changing families. We used to belong to the family of Adam the first man. Now we belong to the family of Christ the true man. For Christ is the Beginner of a new race of men. Death came to mankind through the first Adam's sin, but through the new Adam's obedience we have acquittal and life.

God's forgiving, transforming love, his loving yet demanding concern for us that we call his grace, actually shines all the brighter because of the sin which it destroys. Some people misunderstand this. They go on to say that if grace is God's reaction to sin, if it is such a wonderful experience to be forgiven by God, then let's go on sinning! Not at all. We have been set free—not free *for* sin, but free *from* sin. Once we were "our own men" (as we thought!) but were actually slaves to sin. Now we are slaves of God, and the old master has no rights over us.

And yet we do live in two worlds. I sometimes talk as if Christians did not sin at all. But as an honest Christian I know what it is to have a divided mind. I am still a son of the first Adam, as well as of the Second Adam. I approve things I do not do, and I do things I do not approve. My conscience is better educated than my habits. Sometimes I feel like a healthy man with a corpse chained to his back.

So life is a fight, a fight inside me. But after all, I am Christ's man and I do not belong to sin and death any more. So it is with you and all Christians: Christ lives with you, God's Spirit lives in you; in short, GOD lives in you. That does not make life easy or simple. It does not discharge you from your own private war. You have to put yourself, your worst self, to death, times without number. But you have the spirit of a son now—God's son, not his enemy. We are actually children of God now; we do not have to wait for heaven. Yet we live by hope, for heaven is not here yet. We live by a hope only God can make come true. Meanwhile we know that God works in all things for good with those who love him. It is God who chose us, not we who first chose him. God is *for* us, remember that. He has not let our sins destroy us; he has rescued us, acquitted us, suffered for us, loved us. We have our troubles and tragedies, yes, as long as we live; but nothing—*nothing*—can cut us off from the love of God.

The Problem of the Jews (9:1—11:36)

You might ask me, If all this is so, why are the Jews, your own people, so indifferent to the whole thing? If they are, as you believe, the Number One people of the world when it comes to true religion, why is it that they have not taken to what you call faith? Why can't you persuade your own people?

This question is not only embarrassing, it is tragic. I affirm before God, I would be willing to be shut out from Christ forever if only my people would come to him! It is not a question of my failure to persuade people. I do not believe I ever "converted" a man who was not called by the Holy Spirit first. But that is the problem. Why has the Holy Spirit not stirred the hearts of the Jews with this good news? Has God turned his back on his ancient people?

Only God knows the answer to such questions. It may be that some of the "Israelites" are not part of the true Israel, which may be much smaller than we think, and that only the true Israel will be saved. It may be that God arbitrarily has mercy on some and deliberately makes other men worse. It may be that in some future time Israel will repent and turn to God in Christ as they refuse to do today. What we can surely say is that one great good has come from the Jews' stubbornness and un-faith; namely, the non-Jews have had the good news brought to them. Suppose my own people had given me a full welcome instead of trying to kill me? In that case, at least I would not have turned to the Gentiles as soon as I did. We can also be sure that God has not cast off his ancient people. He will save all Israel somehow, even though how he will or can do this is hid in the mystery of God's all-knowing mind. Though we cannot understand him, let us praise him forever!

Practicing the Life of Faith (12:1—15:13)

Going back to where we were: Please, please don't turn faith into something sentimental, something "spiritual" and out of this world. Bring the life of faith right into the everyday workaday world. Consecrate yourselves to the service of God. Remember you are not expected to be a Christian all by yourself. The whole Christian community should be like one living body, which is healthy only when each member of it is vigorous and active. Be active and enthusiastic in all you do. Do whatever act of kindness is called for. Don't let evil get you down; don't leave a vacuum in your life for evil to rush in. Drive out evil with good. Be good citizens; government is for the good and against the bad. Stay out of debt, I mean in every sense. The only debt you should have is the obligation to love one another—you will never be able to do for others what they have done for you. Remember, love is the great commandment; in fact, love includes all the commandments. Don't get into arguments about details and trifles, such as whether it is right or wrong to eat meat, and whether some days are more sacred than others. In any case avoid doing anything that leads weaker Christians into sin. Faith is the main thing: whatever does not proceed from faith is sin. Christ is our example at all times; live in harmony with one another and with him.

Personal Notes and Benedictions (15:14—16:27)

Of course you know all this, but I have taken the liberty of reminding you before I have the pleasure of seeing you. It is my ambition to tell the good news where no one else has told it, and so I intend to go to Spain soon, and I hope to go by way of Rome and to see you in person.

Give my best wishes to the many Christian people I know in your city. God's peace be with you all, and to God be the glory forever, through Jesus Christ! Amen.

OUTLINE

COMMENTARY

PERSONAL PREFACE

Romans 1:1-15

In ancient times letters began as military communications still do, with the formula:

From:
To:
Subject:

Paul addresses not the "church" but "all God's beloved" in Rome. He does not use the word "church" in this letter till the last chapter, and many interpreters think that chapter 16 did not originally belong with this letter.

For further study, it will be a good project to look through Romans and find what names or expressions Paul uses for Jesus. Here in this short preface, Jesus is referred to as "Christ," as "descended from David," as "Son of God," and as "our Lord." Most remarkable of all is the way Paul puts Christ and God together in his benediction: "Grace . . . and peace from God our Father *and* the Lord Jesus Christ." This is characteristic of Paul's standpoint throughout his writings. Christ is, together with God, the source of our blessings.

You can also have an interesting time putting together what Paul says about Christians in his short but revealing phrases. The first time they are mentioned, here in Romans, they are described as those who were "called to belong to Jesus Christ."

Paul's courtesy is more than formal; it is enthusiastic. With one single exception, every one of his letters pays his readers some high compliments. If Paul sometimes exaggerates, his readers probably did not complain of this habit, and neither should we. Their faith had not been proclaimed in China or the Americas, but they understood what Paul meant. The Christian world had heard of them. Rome was a church and a city "set on a hill," and their light shone far. He compliments them again in 15:14, saying that the Roman Christians are "filled with all knowledge" and that what he wrote was only by way of reminder. But it is clear from the letter itself that he did not mean this literally, and his readers knew oriental courtesy when they heard it.

Paul brings together the different kinds of people who need to have the "good news" of God preached to them: Greeks, barbarians, the wise and the foolish; and also growing Christians. Many Greeks had a high type of religion; "barbarians" generally had low types, and there were wise and foolish people in both classes (1:14-15). Christians need the gospel too. Paul nowhere suggests that his readers were not Christian, or that the first missionaries who started the church at Rome were false teachers. They had been "evangelized"; they had accepted Christ. But evangelism is never quite complete. There is always need to get a better understanding of the faith we have.

THE KEYNOTE: THE RIGHTEOUSNESS OF GOD
Romans 1:16-17

"I am not ashamed" means of course "I am honored," or in the good sense of pride, "I am proud."

The Christian religion, someone has said, always has to come to us from others. It is not something thought out in solitude. It is news; it is something a man left to himself would not be likely to think up. The Christian religion is not first of all good advice, or good habits, or good thoughts, though it includes all of these. It is first of all, *good news*.

But there are different kinds of news. Some news is informing but dull; some is entertaining and amusing but not at all important; some is pleasant enough at the time but fatal in the end. Christianity is *good news of power*. It brings the power of God into life.

Now the "power of God" may be a terrifying thing. It can be shown in ways that blast the beholder. The good news is power "for salvation." What this means will come out in time, for this whole letter is about salvation. A hint is given in the words "righteousness of God." Power, salvation, righteousness—they are all tied together; they are not three separate things, and yet they all either are in the good news or are its results.

But this is true only "through faith for faith." The expression may sound odd and not entirely clear, but one thing *is* clear: this power, salvation, and righteousness do not "work" without faith. Paul makes no explanation, at the moment, of what these words and ideas mean. He simply gives the readers a broad hint of what his letter is going to deal with, namely, the most important issues there are: God, power, salvation, righteousness, faith, life. Not to be interested in these is not to take life seriously. What each of these words means will come out, as we said, by degrees, as Paul gets into his theme.

"The righteous shall live by faith" (margin) or "He who through faith is righteous shall live"; which is it? The Greek can be translated either way. The first translation used to be the standard one; now it is the fashion to use the second translation. They both mean that faith is the foundation of the "righteous" man's life. No righteousness without faith; no true life without faith. At this point we need only say that both translations are true, though Paul's meaning is better expressed by "The righteous shall live by faith" than by a literal translation of Habakkuk 2:4, which would be "The just man shall live by his faithfulness." Paul will come back to this point often.

GOD'S WRATH AND MAN'S SIN
Romans 1:18—3:20

What Sin Is and Does (1:18-32)

Sin as Idolatry

The Christian doctrine of sin is all here in a nutshell. While names of sins and fashions in sins change, sin is always essentially the same in the twentieth century or the first. It begins (1:18-23) with setting up some idol in the place of God. Whatever you can't live without, that is your god. Whatever takes first place with you, whatever you try to please first of all, whatever you sacrifice everything else for, that is your idol.

Once you try to please someone or something instead of the one true God, you are on the downhill road. How far down that road can go, Paul's terrible description in chapter 1 will tell you. He was not making this up; it was a description of life in Corinth, from which he was writing, or in Rome, or in any pagan city in any century.

Paul never says that God has sent or will send people to hell for these or other sins. He says something more terrible: "God gave them up." He just took his hand away and let men do as they pleased. He let them create their own hell, living in the world they preferred to *his* world.

"Well," someone says, "how could God blame the heathen? They didn't know any better."

Paul's answer to that is a short one: they were without excuse, because God's power and deity (Godhood) have been clearly perceived in the things he has made. In other words, the creation speaks to us of its Creator. To take for a god anything less than the Creator is to take the fatal wrong turning.

Sin as Disobedience

Sin cannot be understood apart from God. No atheist can understand sin. Communists do not speak of "right" and "wrong" so much as of "correct" and "incorrect," meaning "what Communism prescribes" and "what Communism forbids." But sin is going against—not a party, not the neighbors, not one's own character or best interests, though it is that, too; sin at its core is *going against God*. This can take place at different levels. Paul does not blame the heathen for not believing in Christ, or for not accepting the Jewish law. He does say they are to blame because they were not *faithful to what they could know of God*. Sin furthermore involves a false start (loyalty to less than the Highest); a wrong road (the way of sin); and a missed goal (coming short of the glory of God).

The Locus of Sin

Where in human life shall we look for the center of sin? Is it in the body, in its instincts, the "ape and tiger" in us? Is it primarily in the sex instinct? Such questions have often been answered in a lump by saying the "locus" or special location of sin is in the physical body, while the soul or spirit is in itself free from sin. But a study of the lists of actual sins mentioned by Paul here and elsewhere (for instance, in Gal. 5) shows that sins of the mind and/or spirit are named right along with sins of the "flesh." Indeed, as we shall see, "flesh" in Paul's thought does not mean flesh-and-blood, as a rule, but is a name for all the anti-God tendencies and desires in a man; indeed, in Paul "flesh" is sometimes used for what is not fleshly, solid-fleshly, at all. The real locus of sin is in the *self*, not exclusively in the physical body.

The Consequence of Sin

The consequence of sin—as we have seen—is just *sin*. The worst penalty for sin is to fall deeper and deeper into it. The worst penalty for sin is to love sin; it is to reach the point where one can no longer tell good from evil. A person can be "adjusted" to sin as he can be to cocaine. People have been "adjusted" to crime; but these are the most dangerous criminals. Whole societies and nations, indeed, have become adjusted to sin, and have thus brought untold disasters on the world. A person who really prefers sin to God, who prefers his own wishes to God's will, does not realize how low he has fallen.

Paul uses a strong word, which he did not invent: the *wrath* of God. This is not vengefulness, not anger; it is nothing like human rage. What Paul means is summed up in those two expressions, "against" (1:18) and "gave . . . up" (1:24, 26, 28). Think—the supreme Power in the universe, *against* what you are doing, determined that you shall fail! The supreme Power leaving you to yourself in silent scorn. . . .

Sin Is Race-Wide (2:1-29)

Many readers of Romans, like many listeners to Paul no doubt, might wish to disagree with him on one point in particular. All that you say of sin is true, they might say, but it is not true of everybody. There are many persons (they would say) who have high ideals, who look down on and despise the low and vulgar sinners. They have the same disgust that you have for the kind of sins you were describing. Furthermore, what about the Jews? They have the highest type of religion ever known. Besides, they are your own people. It is all very well to condemn the masses of men; they are a sorry lot. But not the high-minded, not the Jews, surely!

Paul speaks to the first point (concerning men of moral insight and ideals) in chapter 2:1-16, and to the second point (about the Jews) in 2:17—3:20. It is true, he does not fully explain his argument, nor logically prove it. He just tosses out the hand grenade and lets the splinters hit where they will. (This may be one of the places where he leaves it up to the intelligent reader to decide on the merits of the case.)

What Paul says is that the moral critic is guilty of the same sins for which he attacks others. Jesus brought this out in the Sermon on the Mount (Matt. 5-7) and in his verdicts on the Pharisees (Matt. 23; Luke 11:37-44). Even the Romans had a proverb: "Every man carries two sacks; one in front for his neighbor's faults and one behind for his own." It is only the moral critic who thinks he is perfect; no one else shares his admiration for himself. The man who despises the "gross" or obvious sinner, the hoodlum or scoundrel, may easily be guilty of sins which—in comparison with his ideals—are worse than those of the ignorant hoodlum.

One difficult point in this section has to do with 2:6-16. Does Paul contradict himself here? Right in the middle of his argument he speaks of a future judgment at which God will "render to every man according to his works" (vs. 6). People who write books on Romans have struggled manfully with this passage. At two crucial points it does not fit Paul's teaching about faith and righteousness (not only in Romans but elsewhere): (1) he speaks of eternal life as a reward for "patience in well-doing" (vs. 7); and (2) he assumes that some men do actually do what the Law requires. One general opinion is that this passage must be understood in conformity with Paul's more usual teaching, which is that God approves or disapproves men according to their faith, not their "works." Another opinion is that this passage weakens the insistence on justification "by faith alone," and that other passages should be understood in conformity with this one. Still other interpreters believe that this is a kind of ironic passage. Just as a certain Irishman was reported as saying, "I believe in hell, because the Church teaches it; but by the mercy of God there's nobody in it," so Paul may be saying: "Everyone who does good will receive eternal life; but because of the sinfulness of man, nobody can claim it on that basis." Others have written that what Paul is trying to say is that God is impartial, and deals with Jew and Gentile alike on the same basis.

In 2:25-29 Paul deals with circumcision, which marked off the Jewish man from the non-Jewish. Many Jews came to regard this rite as a kind of magic, whereby a true Jew could get past all difficulties and through all doors and pass an examination at the Last Judgment with flying colors. Paul's point about it is that circumcision does not serve as a label of a true Jew; that is a matter of the heart. The Jews were, by God's intention, God's people; but the cold fact is that many of them were not really his. One can say in modern language that Church membership is good, provided the Church member is a real Christian. But being baptized does not in itself make one a Christian.

Are Jews a Special Case? (3:1-20)

As for the Jew, Paul would have been the first to claim that
the Jewish religion was the true religion, or at any rate that the
Jews worshiped the one true God. They also had the highest
moral standards in the Roman world. Paul will come back again
and again to discuss the Jews; he was much more interested in
them than most Gentile readers of this letter are. But he is
mainly concerned about them as examples of the best religion
there is, *apart from Christ*.

He even suggests that they are actually worse than the Gentiles,
because the Jews had had the Law of God to go by in a way and
at a level different from that of the Gentiles. A homemade do-
it-yourself medicine man in the backwoods can be blamed for
killing people with his mixtures; but he is not nearly so much to
blame as the graduate in pharmacy who makes a mistake he was
taught never to make. The more you know, the more you are to
blame; that is common sense, and Paul applies it to the Jews.

Three sentences we may set down as summing up the main
points of this part of Romans are: all men have sinned (3:10-12);
all men are in the grip of sin (3:9); and, most discouraging of
all, no human being can get God's approval even by doing what
God requires (3:20). (For the *why* of this, see the comment on
3:21—4:25.)

JUSTIFICATION BY FAITH

Romans 3:21—4:25

The Problem

The word "justify" sounds dry to a newcomer. It has a legalistic
sound, for it belongs to the jargon of ancient courtrooms. It is so
much associated with the name of Paul that some people think
justification was his hobby, a doctrine his lawyer mind invented.
But the word is neither dry nor is it Paul's special hobby. Justification is one of many figures of speech that Christians
have long used. But it is nobody's hobby. It represents a universal problem, one with which every religion in the world, past

or present, is in some way concerned. Indeed, it is the most vital question any man can face. People who cannot spell the word and who have never heard of it, may ask themselves the chilling question, "How do I stand with God?" Chilling, because the suspicion creeps into the mind, "I haven't *any* standing with him!"

Frankly, if we treated any ordinary person as it is our habit to treat God—working against his interests most of the time, indifferent to him the rest of the time, never listening to what he says to us, speaking to him only by way of an occasional scream for help—if we treated people that way we would have no friends. How can God accept us as friends?

"Working against his interests" is putting it much too mildly. We work against *him,* we resist *him.* Practically, we demand his resignation as God and we set up ourselves—our own desires, judgments, plans, comforts, even whims—set up our shabby selves as The Most Important Object in the universe. We act as though we thought him stupid, for we think we are deceiving him as easily as we fool our grandmothers; we even act as though we thought him bad, for we expect him to let us get away with murder. Yet we *want* him on our side. In serious moments we know that if he is not, we are lost. We are like a man who wants to be reconciled to his wife but perversely keeps on doing and saying insulting things that only drive her further away. How can God accept us?

"Justification" can be given other names. Paul himself was not tied to any one set of words. The question, How can God justify the unjust? can be asked in other ways: How can God forgive the unforgivable? How can God accept the unacceptable? How can God reconcile the unreconcilable?

That is the problem of justification. Of course there are people who are not bothered by it in the least. Nevertheless it is a real problem, and it becomes acute when it gets into the first person singular. How can *I* come to terms with God?

False Solutions

We may understand Paul's answer to this problem better if we take a quick look at other answers. First, we know there are many who do not see the problem. We cannot appreciate it at all unless (1) we believe in a God who is entirely good, whose will is always good; and (2) we have consciences that tell us that we are not fit for God's approval. But let us assume that a man does believe in God, and has a working conscience, even a primitive one. Then what?

The Epicureans would have said there is no problem. Not because God does not exist, but because God, or the gods, just does not care. An ant in the woods is not bothered about his standing with you; he goes his way and you go yours, and you do not care. But all high religions understand that God *does* care, and we have to take him seriously or suffer the consequences.

The kind of high religion represented by the Greek writer of tragedies, Aeschylus, understood well the "wrath of God" on greatly wicked men, but he saw no outcome except the pursuing and destructive vengeance of a God who could not be appeased.

In some very popular misinterpretations of religion—including a common misunderstanding of the Hebrew religion—it was considered impossible to please God by doing what he requires, since his requirements were too strenuous. So God had provided, it was thought, an easier way, the way of sacrifice. In this view not everybody could keep the Ten Commandments, but anybody who could afford it could offer up a lamb, or have a priest do it for him. Sacrifice thus would become a substitute for obedience. (Isaiah 1 and Micah 6:6-8 show how the prophets protested against this parody of religion.)

The kind of Jew that Paul had been before his conversion, took this matter most seriously of all. He believed that God had set forth his will in his Law, and that the way to God's approval, the way to have the right standing in God's sight, was to keep the Law. As simple as that!

The trouble with this was twofold. On the one hand it led straight into the conceit and complacency of the Pharisees. Many "trusted in themselves that they were righteous and despised others" (Luke 18:9), and Jesus had little use for them. Pride is the blight that withers the flower of virtue.

On the other hand—and especially for a man like Paul, a man with a high sense of God and a keen conscience—this method of winning God's favor by building up a kind of ladder out of "works of law" simply leads to despair. Unlike the kind of Pharisee whom Jesus denounced, this kind of man knows he does *not* keep the Law—that is, carry out the will of God to perfection—and yet he feels that unless he does so he will never win God's approval. God's verdict is always "Guilty," and it is small comfort to know that this is God's verdict on every man. How Paul discovered the key to the riddle, the answer to the problem, we do not fully know. But the answer he gave in this letter not only appealed to the church at Rome (for we know that the Christians there kept and treasured the letter), but in time appealed to the whole Church. It was not merely one man's idea; it was the truth, a truth which God wanted his children to know, a truth for all times and all men.

The True Solution (3:21-31)

In Paul's words, "A man is justified by faith apart from works of law" (3:28). God's approval, his "justification," his verdict of acquittal, his forgiveness, a right standing with him—this is not to be bought, it cannot be earned. Men are "justified by his grace as a gift" (3:24).

Once get this straight and you have the clue to the Christian life; you have also a leading truth which is related to most of what Paul has yet to say. For although this, in a sense, is the main theme of the letter, it raises a great many questions, which Paul proceeds to deal with.

Someone might ask: So God really makes no requirements of us? If his grace is a gift, then we need not do a thing! On the contrary, there is one thing that is required: *faith*. But faith is not a thing you do, it is not a virtue you practice. Faith is accepting God's acceptance of us in Christ. It is letting God take our hand and lift us up. Faith is not just another form of currency, so to speak, by which to buy God's grace. Faith is not a good-deed-to-end-all-good-deeds, for which we are suitably rewarded.

There is a somewhat short and mysterious glimpse here of what is brought out elsewhere in Paul's writings and in the rest of the New Testament; namely, that God's grace is connected with the death of Jesus Christ. Just what this connection is cannot be seen directly from this passage (3:24-25).

But Paul uses two suggestive words here, "redemption" and "expiation." Each is a figure of speech drawn from the Old Testament. We may note that "redemption" is an idea going back to the time when if a Hebrew got taken over as a slave, for debt or otherwise, his next of kin was expected to buy him free. This suggests that Christ, so to speak, bought sinners free from their slavery to sin, and that the price he paid was his own life.

"Expiation" is one of the meanings of "sacrifice," a word not used here. If we may get ahead of our story, we can say that in many places in the New Testament, not only in Paul, Christ's death is considered a sacrifice. Paul refers to Christ's death in this way (I Cor. 5:7; Eph. 5:2) and also to his blood as sacrificial (Rom. 5:9; I Cor. 10:16; Eph. 1:7; 2:13; Col. 1:20).

Sacrifice is a complex problem, but it is clear that in the Old Testament the word had many meanings and intentions. The Early Church, following Paul's lead, singled out one of these as basic—namely, substitution. The one who made a sacrifice of a living animal imaginatively identified himself with the sacrifice. The killing of the beast signified the wrath of God; in other words, the repenting man felt he deserved to die—the universe would be better off if his own bad life were destroyed. But God allowed him to make the sacrifice as a substitute for himself. The purpose was not simply to wipe the slate clean, it was to give him a fresh start and restore him to fellowship with God. So Christ above all is the final and all-availing sacrifice which brings sinning man back to God. Note that it is God who "puts forward" Jesus; in other words, the death of Jesus did not change God from anger to love. It is the loving God who makes the sacrifice possible.

In verses 27-31 Paul repeats the thought that justification, right relation to God, is not something to boast about, as did the Pharisee in Jesus' parable (Luke 18:9-14), for such a relationship cannot be managed, bought, earned, or deserved on our side. God alone can make it possible. This is true for Jews, true for non-Jews.

The Example of Abraham (4:1-25)

Paul as a good Jew was particularly interested in Abraham. The main point of chapter 4 is that Abraham was "justified" by faith; in other words, that the reason for his standing with God —which no Jew would deny was a high one—was not that he was so good or obedient; his basic relation to God was one of *faith*. In 4:3 Abraham's faith is described—"Abraham believed God." Paul is not claiming that Abraham was a Christian. He does claim that Abraham's faith was the central feature of his relationship to God.

Abraham makes a first-class example, because you could take

him as a type of both Jew and non-Jew. He was a Jew in the
sense that he was the "father of his country," the original patri-
arch, the founder of the race and the religion. Yet he was a
Gentile in that he lived long before Moses, he came out of a non-
Jewish background (where could he have found a Jewish background?), his father had been an idol-worshiper (Joshua 24:2).

What had endeared Abraham to God? Not his keeping the
Law; the Law had not yet been given. Not circumcision; when
God first made a covenant with Abraham, the rite of circumcision had not been performed. So, as Paul puts it, he was "the
father of all who believe without being circumcised"—the Gentiles; "and likewise the father of the circumcised who are not
merely circumcised but also follow the example of the faith
which . . . Abraham had"—Jews who believe in Christ. Paul
does not say that Abraham believed in Christ. What he does insist upon is that Abraham's relation to God was not based on anything he had done, but on that simple trust in God, apart from
any claims, which we call faith.

Note that Paul sometimes speaks of faith in Jesus (3:26) and
sometimes of faith in God (4:24). This is another of the ways in
which he almost merges God and Christ. At any rate, it would
not be stretching the truth to say that for Paul, we are saved by
faith in Jesus, or faith in God; it does not really matter which.
How can you have faith in one without having faith in the other,
he would ask.

A present-day Christian may wonder why Paul spends a whole
chapter on Abraham, and why he repeats himself so often (for
the argument is really finished with verse 12). This is because of the kind of argument which Paul must have met in the
synagogues many a time, and which he assumed would be raised
at Rome. A Jew who could not see Paul's point would think
something like this: "See here, what is the difference between us
Jews and the rest of the world? Why are we God's Chosen People? It is this: We are the People of the Law. We began by Law;
we live by Law; we alone, of all the peoples of the earth, know
what God wants and we alone do it. Yes, even Abraham, though
he lived long before Moses, did as God commanded him. It's
perfectly simple: Obey God and he will reward you. All this talk
Paul gives us about 'faith' is morally upsetting. What you get
from God depends on what you do, not on what you think."

Against that sort of argument, Paul is making these points:

(1) Faith is not a way of thinking. It is not a "believing-that," it is a "believing-in." It is throwing oneself, so to speak, into the arms and the mercy of God. (2) If right relation with God depended on law, the Jews would get nowhere with it, because though they do know the Law after a fashion, they don't keep it; and the Gentiles would get nowhere because they don't even know the Law.

This is not all an old, forgotten debate. Don't we know people who have no use for the Church because they "don't need it"? Aren't there people who think religion is not for the healthy-minded? They may not put it quite this way to themselves, but it boils down to this: "I suit myself all right. So God had better be suited with me, if he's reasonable! I don't want favors of God, I don't ask for charity, all I want is my rights." Paul has already shown that this leaves us out in the dark. If we insist on "law"—that is, being good and doing good *as a condition* of God's favorable attitude toward us—we are sunk, because God's standard is nothing short of perfection. So it's either faith or nothing.

Of course there was still the objection that faith destroys law, that faith gives license to do as we please. Paul denies this in 3:31 and elsewhere; but the real case for the proposition that faith does not upset morals or throw character overboard is in all that Paul says, in this and other letters, about Christian conduct. The life based on faith is actually of a higher quality than life based merely on law. But more of this later on. (See the comment on chapter 12 and following.)

RESULTS OF JUSTIFICATION AND REFLECTIONS ON THE LIFE OF THE CHILDREN OF GOD
Romans 5:1—8:39

The next chapters present many difficulties, but two bits of advice may help. First, in reading here or elsewhere, even if you do not understand all of it, and even if commentaries only make confusion worse, remember there is much here which is not only true but beautiful and clear. Stick to what you do understand, for the present, and let what you do not understand come later. Second, Paul is not the systematic kind of writer who lays his ideas out in neat packages, going through one at a time. His

thought moves not so often in a straight line as in spirals. The
same ideas come back again and again, at different levels.

What Christ Has Done for Us (5:1-21)

You will find it worth while to write down, not only in chapter
5 but through the whole letter, what is said about what Christ
has done for us: "Through him we have obtained access to this
grace . . . Christ died for the ungodly . . . died for us . . . we are
now justified by his blood . . ." and so on. Paul seldom if ever
puts all his teaching on any subject into one chapter, but this
chapter gives us a good opportunity to set down a few truths
about what Christ has done for us.

1. Christ's life, death, and resurrection were *for us* and not
for himself. If you want one word for it, Christ's life and death
were vicarious. This is partly true of all good human lives; su-
premely true of Jesus.

2. What Christ has done is what God has done in him. God
sent Christ; God was *in* Christ. It is not true that Christ by his
mercy warded off the anger of God. God's mercy produced
Christ; Christ did not create mercy in God.

3. Justification (God's approval, the verdict that sets sin's
prisoner free) is possible because God sees us in Christ. As Paul
grew older he used the expression "in Christ" more and more
often. It has been said that "in Christ" is *the* typical and central
idea of Paul. God looks at us as if he were actually looking at
Christ himself.

4. None of this is anything we can achieve; we can only accept
it. A phrase often used in the Church is "the finished work of
Christ." There is a finished and an unfinished work of Christ.
Some babies have been born since you started reading this page.
If any of them become Christians, Christ will be at work in them.
That work has hardly been begun, much less finished. Christ's
work *in* you is not finished in your lifetime. But Christ's work *for*
you is finished. There is a once-for-all-ness about Jesus. There
was only one of him; there was only one miracle of Christmas,
only one Life, only one Death, only one Resurrection. And this
is for us—if we accept it. Even if we do not accept it, it is still
for us; but it has no more saving effect, without acceptance, than
if it had not happened.

At this point let us stop for an important parenthesis. The

Christian faith is founded on fact, but facts alone do not make Christian faith. A fact, in the scientific sense, is something expressed by a proposition that cannot reasonably be doubted. "Christ died" refers to a fact. It was a visible fact; no one has ever doubted it—except those very few who doubt that he even lived! But when Paul says, "Christ died for us," he is doing more than stating a fact; he is interpreting a fact. Now both the fact and the interpretation are vital. The interpretation is meaningless without the fact. If Christ did *not* die, then of course his death could not be for us. But if all we can say is that he died, then his death means no more than the death of anyone else. But "for us" is not a fact in the scientific sense, and we should not either pretend that it is or mourn because it is not. Indeed it is the "for us" or "for me" that faith accepts. Accepting the mere fact of Christ's death is accepting a "vital statistic" and has no religious value. But to accept as true the interpretation "for us," can change life.

But how do we know that it *is* true? Can truths never be tested, as facts can? Do we have to take them or leave them? Truths can be tested, or many of them can be, but in quite a different way from facts. A fact can be checked in a laboratory, or by eyewitnesses. A truth is not checked in a laboratory; it is tested in life. Truths are such large things that a laboratory is too small a place to test them. A statement of a fact, such as "two and two make four," can be tested on a small piece of paper. A statement of more complicated fact, such as what coal is made of, can be tested in a laboratory. But "two are better than one" is a truth that needs the breadth of life for testing, and indeed some truths are so great as to need not only this life but the life everlasting to give us the complete demonstration. Do you believe that Christ died "for us"? That we are reconciled to God through his death? The way to test this truth is to live by it and at last to die by it.

Peace, Joy, Reconciliation, and Love (5:1-11)

Paul now begins in chapter 5 to speak of the results in life of "justification by faith"; and these are, as already said, results of the truths on which faith lays hold. Indeed it would be better to say that faith simply opens the door to God, letting God take over.

There has been a great deal of argument about the first verse here (5:1). Some of the best and oldest of the handwritten copies of the Greek text of this verse have "let us have peace," and other equally ancient and reliable copies read "we have peace." It seems more in line with Paul's general thought to take this as a statement of fact: we do have peace with God. The war is over. God has come more than halfway to meet us; he has come *all* the way. He has offered himself to us in Jesus Christ. If there is hostility between us, it is not the fault of God, and it never was. The Battle of New Orleans was fought actually after the peace treaty between England and the United States had been signed. The battle was needless. So there is a kind of implied "let us have peace" wrapped up in "we have peace." Since God is at peace with us, let us live as men who know that this is true.

The Christian life is also one of joy. Three levels of joy can be seen here: rejoicing in hope, in sufferings, in God (5:2, 3, 11). This hope is not hope that tomorrow will be a better day, or that the law of averages will one day give us a break. It is the tremendous hope of "sharing the glory of God" (vs. 2). Paul seldom speaks of heaven; his word for the final stage, the future that cannot be imagined, the life beyond this one, is "glory." What it will be to "share" the divine glory our minds cannot imagine, but our hearts leap up when we think of it.

We rejoice in suffering not because pain in itself is good, but because it is the engraver's tool with which God creates lines of beauty on the life.

Most difficult it is to rejoice in God. The least this can mean is rejoicing in what gives God joy. What can we say of a person who really does not care for any of the things God likes? If such a person is a "Christian" he will most certainly be a gloomy one. And if God seems too far away for us to understand him, then note that Paul puts in "rejoice in God through our Lord Jesus Christ" (vs. 11). We do know, as a matter of fact, what gave Jesus joy and satisfaction. If we learn from him, we shall find ourselves more and more seeing life as he saw it, rejoicing in God through him.

We have already glanced at reconciliation in a previous section. It will do the Christian reader good to think over his own life and reflect how much of it is lived as if God were a stranger, or an enemy. Notice also that Paul does not speak of God's becoming reconciled to us but of God's reconciling us to himself. We do not force reconciliation on God; we accept his love and grace in the grace and love of Christ, who "is our peace" (Eph. 2:14).

Adam and Christ (5:12-24)

Part of Paul's originality, and what makes reading him interesting, is his gift of seeing a resemblance where no one else would
think of it. Adam and Christ—how unlike they are! How can we
compare Christ to poor, ignorant, stumbling, sinful Adam? Paul
can see the contrast and indeed underscores it. Adam brought
death into the race of man; Christ brought life. But all the same,
Paul sees in Christ a Second Adam. Each is the beginning of a
race; the first Adam the father of all the sinners of the world, the
second the "first-born" (Rom. 8:29) of all the new humanity, the
true sons of God. Indeed, it has been pointed out that if we want
to know what man is, it is much more profitable to look at Jesus
than at Adam. Adam was the human being who cracked up (and
"everybody's middle name is Adam"); Christ is the Human Being who did not crack up. Adam was the man who fled from
God; Christ is the Man in whose face we see the light of the glory
of God (II Cor. 4:6). In more prosaic language, Jesus is the
truly *normal*—that is to say, standard—human being. To become
like him, to belong (if one may say so) to his family rather than
to that of Adam the First, is not to become freakish and ab-
normal; it is to discover what being human really is.

Freedom from Sin (6:1-11)

Paul has been accused, in his lifetime and ever since, of saying
some things he never said, or meaning what he never meant.
There have been, for example, people who have totally misunderstood his teaching about "faith" and "grace."

Their argument goes something like this: If it is true that we
cannot build a ladder to heaven out of good deeds, what is the use
of being or doing good at all? And if it is true that God's grace is
free, and that he is gracious because he is good, why not keep on
committing sins, to give him a chance to be gracious? "God will
forgive; that's his business," said a mocking Frenchman. (See the
section on "Anti-law 'Christianity' " in the Introduction.)

But God is not a vast forgiving-machine. There is no such
thing as justification all by itself. To use another technical word
which is also a Bible word, justification when it is real always is
welded to sanctification. It is a good thing the Letter to the Romans did not end with chapter 4; if it had, there would have
been some excuse for misunderstanding Paul. In chapter 5 it be-

gins to be clearer, and in chapter 6 it becomes clear beyond any mistake, that justification is not a mere legal fiction; there is something vital, powerful, about it. The courtroom word is useful but it is not nearly rich enough to express the whole truth about the Christian life.

In grammar, the indicative mood states facts, the imperative mood gives commands. If chapter 5 gives some indicatives of the Christian's life-in-grace, chapter 6 gives some imperatives of grace.

Before Paul comes to these imperatives, he gives us some more indicatives. He uses odd language, for he is dealing with life as it is in God, and this is far from commonplace. Observe: We were buried with Christ by baptism; we were united with him in a death like his, we have died with Christ; but as Christ was raised, so it is with us. (Paul shows that he knows that the full and final reality of this is yet to be.) We left sin behind us when we died; the Christian life is a *new* life. It is the life of heaven brought to earth. This is a long way from courtroom thinking. It is thinking in an entirely new dimension.

Perhaps we can understand it if we think about what we may call the principle of "identification." We see it in everyday life. "Any friend of yours is a friend of mine" is one example of it. True sympathy is another. A mother suffers when her children suffer, she feels shame if they are disgraced, she rejoices when they are praised. That is identification.

It is interwoven with the Christian life; indeed, apart from identification, the Christian life dries up to something powerless, something merely formal—a matter of words, not reality. We can see three different but interlinked identifications in the whole process of the Christian life. One is the identification of Christ and God; they are never precisely the same, yet they cannot be separated. We have seen that Christ's life and death was God's act, not less than Jesus' own. The love and the grace of God are not to be thought of as different from the love and grace of Christ. The second is Christ's identification of himself with sinners. Beginning with his baptism and going right through the Crucifixion, he made himself one with sinful men. Then there is one more identification without which the first bears no fruit: the identification by the sinner of himself with Christ, or rather the acceptance of this identification which Christ has made. A Christian life may begin at a deep level when a person looking at the Cross feels and knows: "This is for me. I belong there; he took my place." But the Christian also looks at the risen Christ, and says, "There am I." Christ was tempted before his resurrection; never afterward. He had passed beyond sin's gravitation; he was already in the orbit of heaven. So it is with the Christian.

The Imperatives of Grace (6:12-23)

But wait: is this realistic? Did you ever know any Christian who had actually, as Paul puts it, died to sin, been entirely set free from it? You never did, and neither did Paul. We have to help make the heavenly reality come true. It is not automatic, it is not magic. And it never comes completely true in this life. To the very people to whom he had just said, "You also must consider yourselves dead to sin" (6:11), Paul says, *therefore* "Let not sin ... reign ... Do not yield your members to sin." He writes, "You ... have become obedient from the heart to the standard of teaching to which you were committed" (vs. 17). The Christian is not free to do as he pleases. God gives him a standard to live by. There are divine imperatives for the Christian.

Paul uses also the figure of master and slave. The Christian is not to be defined as a person who cannot sin, or who never sins. A Christian is one who is no longer a slave of sin. He is no longer in chains. He is God's man, not sin's man. And, Paul asks, what does sin do for you? Nothing; it kills you in the end. Sin pays you off—with death. God does much better than pay you. He *gives* you—eternal life.

The Divided Life (7:1-25)

In chapter 6 Paul speaks of the Christian's freedom from sin. In chapter 7 he speaks of our freedom from the Law. First, we need to understand what "law" he means, and then to see what importance this has for the ordinary twentieth-century Christian. He does not mean by "law" the statutes of any city or of a state. He does not mean "natural law" such as the law of gravitation, or the law of self-preservation. Here, as always, he means *the* Law as all Jews would understand it, the "Law of Moses"— what we find in the Books of Exodus through Deuteronomy. However, as he speaks of Law in this chapter, he does not mean all those laws. Some of them, for example, concerned priests only; no ordinary Jew could be tempted to break them, for the same reason that you are not tempted to break the laws governing the behavior of royalty. Paul is speaking of the Law at its highest level and broadest reach, the "moral law," summed up in the Ten Commandments.

But the problem he is about to raise is not for Jews only. In the first place, the Law (in this sense) was understood then, and still is, to be intended for all mankind. The Ten Commandments are by no means a private set of bylaws for a small minority of the human race. In the second place, here as elsewhere Paul uses the Jews and their moral-religious problems as a prime example of all that is best in the moral-religious world. If the approach to God by way of the "Jewish" Law proved to be a failure, all other approaches along the same line would fail. We have already seen (in chapter 5) how Paul shows that winning God's favor by the way of living up to life's highest ideals (in the Jews' case, living up to the Law) simply will not do, just because the ideals are out of reach. If any reader thinks the Ten Commandments can be easily observed, he should study what Jesus said in the Sermon on the Mount (Matt. 5).

So all this applies to us, that is, if we are high-minded and have high ideals. If Paul seems to be hard on ideals, remember that for him the Law of God in the Scripture was the highest ideal there was or could be. It was an ideal that had been set up by no less an authority than God himself. So what Paul has to say about the Law and our relation to it must at first have sounded rather shocking to his Jewish readers, for it shocks us when we substitute for the word "law" the words "man's highest ideals."

Dead to the Law (7:1-12)

Paul, at least in the beginning of this section (vss. 1-6), keeps on with the thought that we have died and risen again with Christ. Just as we have died to sin, we have died to the Law (vs. 4). His metaphors are a little mixed, but his meaning is clear. You were wedded to the Law, he says, and there was no ground for divorce; it had every claim on you. But now that you have died and been raised, you are set free by death.

This is a good thing, because as long as you were under the Law you were being constantly stimulated to sin. Paul here goes into a sort of parenthesis: If law suggests lawbreaking, as of course it often does, then is not the Law to blame? Not at all, he says. Paul gets support at this point from a nontheologian, Mark Twain. This plain-spoken American said that most idealists overlooked one feature of the human make-up which is very prominent, namely, plain mulishness or perverseness. Mark Twain said that if a mule thinks he knows what you want him to do he will do just the opposite, and Twain admitted he was like that himself—often mean for the sake of meanness. But the fault lies not in the ideal but in the man who reacts against it. It is sin, Paul says, that killed me, not the holy, just, and good Law of God.

The Divided Life (7:13-25)

This is one of the plainest parts of Paul's letters and yet one that causes an endless lot of arguments. Still, no one can miss the meaning. Verse 19 sums it up: "I do not do the good I want, but the evil I do not want is what I do." Life is divided; we serve the Law of God and the law of sin at the same time. Mind and flesh are at war with each other. There is in me something that wants to do right, that rejoices in God's will. There is something also that hates to do right, and drags me back to the slavery of sin. Am I good or bad? Am I good because I so heartily approve what is good, or bad because my performance is never up to my ideal?

What people who study Romans argue about is not the meaning of this passage in itself, but the question: Who is talking? Is this the converted, committed Christian, dead to sin, living the "new life of the Spirit" (7:6); or is it the old sinner? Is this autobiographical? If it is, is it Saul before his conversion, or Paul afterwards? The strongest reason for taking this passage (vss. 13-25) as a description of a pre-Christian experience is that in the light of all that Paul has said up to now about the Christian life, it is strange that he should describe it in terms of a divided—and indeed defeated—existence. If this represents the Christian life, the argument runs, then what an ineffective thing faith is! What good is it to be Christian if this is all that can be said of it?

On the other hand, there are some strong reasons for taking this passage to refer to the Christian. For one thing, why would Paul, without warning the reader, go back into picturing life as it is without Christ? Has he not been talking of the Christian life ever since chapter 4 at least? For another thing, does this not describe the Christian's life as it actually often is? Is it not true that the best of men have their worse sides? A third point is that this passage, more vividly than most, is saying what Paul always sees in the best Christians he knows: there are no perfect saints. In every letter but one he heaps what seems to be extravagant praise on his Christian friends, and then proceeds almost at once to condemn their sins (see comment on 1:1-15).

The reader should try to make up his own mind about this. He will have plenty of company, no matter how he decides. Two more thoughts may cast some light on it. One, going back to chapter 5, is that although we now, as Christians, belong to the family of Christ, we still cannot deny that we are of Adam's race too. Adam is the man of yesterday, Christ the Man of all tomorrows. Adam, so to speak, is pulling us back into the shadows; Christ is drawing us forward into light. The other thought is that although Paul is describing a divided life, it is not for that reason a defeated life. It comes out in victory, through Christ the Deliverer (vss. 24-25).

"More Than Conquerors" in Christ (8:1-39)

The eighth chapter of Romans is easily one of the finest chapters in the whole Bible. In many ways it is the climax of this letter. It calls for meditation in a devotional mood rather than for cool analysis. You will have no serious difficulty with it. It is this and similar passages in Paul which show that for him theology was nothing dry, designed only for specialists.

Merely to start the reader's thoughts, it may be pointed out that this chapter furnishes a wealth of ways of describing the Christian life. Among these are: a life of freedom from the law of sin and death (vs. 2); a "walk" according to (that is, in harmony with) the Spirit (vs. 4); a mind centered in what pleases God ("things of the Spirit") (vs. 5); a life "in" the Spirit—with God, so to speak, the very atmosphere we breathe (vs. 9); being a home for the Spirit of God (vs. 9); being a home for Christ (vs. 10); being fully alive, in body and spirit (vss. 10-11); an execution of the old bad self (vs. 13); being sons of God—and his heirs, along with Christ (vs. 17); a life that shares Christ's sufferings (vs. 18); a life of hope (vss. 24-25); a life of prayer (vss. 26-27); a life of assurance (vss. 28-30); a life of conquest over all trials and all enemies (vss. 31-39).

Right in the midst of the most eloquent flights comes the word "predestined" twice (vss. 29-30). This is another word which theologians have battled over; but you should note the company in which this word appears, and the mood which brings it out. It appears in a series beginning with the great affirmation, "We know that in everything God works for good with those who love him" (vs. 28). The center of thought here is the amazing and undeserved goodness of God. Then comes the series: purpose—foreknowledge—predestination—calling—justification—glorification. Predestination here points to God's *plan* by which his *purpose* is carried out. A God who wishes well is not enough. A God who wishes well but has no plan by which to make his wishes come true would be a very feeble God.

Predestination here appears as a reason for rejoicing and confidence, not for puzzlement and doubt. It is connected with good, not evil; indeed, nowhere in the New Testament is the word "predestine" used to express a purpose of, or toward, evil.

Predestination also points to God's choosing us rather than our choosing him. Jesus often spoke of the life of glory as a feast, a banquet. Those who are present cannot say, "I invited myself," but rather, "I was invited."

If anyone worries about whether he is predestined or not—predestined to glory—it is a pretty sure sign that he *is* predestined. But coming back to Paul, it is unfair to him to take predestination away from the series where he puts it. Those who are predestined are called. Anyone who has ever felt the call of God—not "call" in the sense of a call to the ministry, say, but a call to faith, to the "life in Christ"—may be sure he is predestined; in other words, the call he has felt was not an accident. God intended it, he planned it so.

This eighth chapter is the great chapter on the Holy Spirit; in all of Paul's writings there is none which says more concerning the Spirit than this does. The reader can begin making his own "doctrine of the Holy Spirit," if he likes, by putting together all that is said here about the Spirit. Note that Paul does not try to explain *who* and *why* the Spirit is, but concentrates on what the Spirit *does*. You can start with this obvious point: the Holy Spirit is never spoken of in the New Testament as a vague cloudy sort of *It*, but as a vital and personal Power.

In the Revised Standard Version the word "adoption" occurs only in Romans 8:23 and Galatians 4:5; the same Greek word is translated "sonship" or "to be his sons" in Romans 8:15; 9:4; and Ephesians 1:5. It is now, as it was then, a legal word. Does it indicate that our sonship to God, and his Fatherhood, are no more than legal fictions? Does it suggest that our relation to God is something artificial, not natural? By no means. We have to think what this word would mean to Roman readers. Two points stand out. First, an adopted child is a chosen child. Paul's use of the word shows that he is thinking of God's *choosing* his children; they are his children by his deliberate will.

Second, in Roman usage an adopted child was by no means a second-class son, a son by legal fiction. Roman emperors would adopt young men or boys and appoint them their successors, to the exclusion of their flesh-and-blood sons. It was felt by the Romans that an adopted son might have more of the father's spirit and might carry on his work better than a natural son.

THE PROBLEM OF GOD'S OWN PEOPLE— THE JEWS
Romans 9:1—11:36

The three chapters 9-11 are notoriously the most difficult in Romans, and among the most difficult in the New Testament. It is a different case from the difficulties in earlier chapters, say 1-4. The trouble there was in accepting what Paul plainly says, as for instance that all men have sinned, and that God's grace is free; and in some later chapters, as in chapter 6, the problem is how to understand a statement which is obviously not literally true, as, for instance, that we have been crucified with Christ. The difficulty with the chapters now before us is that it is hard to put together what Paul says in one consistent straightforward line of thought; in short, it is hard to know what he meant to say. Some commentators will take one verse or passage and build everything around it, making everything else fit; other commentators will do the same with other verses. The conclusion presented here is not new but seems to lessen the difficulties considerably. Again we wish we had the writer of Romans with us to answer all our questions!

Let us suppose, then, that Paul is faced by a very severe problem; but that instead of giving a flat, clear, happy answer to it, or even one profound and troubling answer, he wrestles with the problem, thinking out loud as it were, letting his readers share his thoughts. In this way he arrives at not less than eight different answers to his problem, all possible, but perhaps none of them final unless it is the last one—though even that does not answer all the questions.

A Problem with Different Solutions

For the modern reader, these three chapters make a kind of parenthesis. If they were not here, few would miss them. One can skip from the end of chapter 8 to the beginning of chapter 12 and feel no particular break. For Paul, however, these chapters are no parenthesis. Fond as he was of parentheses and side remarks, he would not have spent nearly a third of his available space on a parenthesis.

The problem, for him, and for the people about whom he is thinking all through these chapters, is an acute one. Has God failed with the Jews? Has he cast them off? What is wrong with them? Are they going to be finally lost? Paul takes it for granted that his readers are well aware of a fact which galled him to the bone: the Jews as a whole had not responded to the gospel. It was not that they were unresponsive; they were actively hostile. They had thrown him out of their synagogues, slandered him, browbeaten his converts, plotted against his life—and the end was not yet. Why was this? They were God's Chosen People (9:4-5 shows how Paul felt about that), and yet they could not accept God's Son. They were God's people, yet they had turned against God's mercy. How to account for this almost incredible state of things, and what to think about the future of the Jews, constitute the problem for Paul. The four questions raised above are all mixed together, and make up the one big question: What about the Jews? (Paul uses the old sentimental name "Israel.")

Paul begins with the implied fact of the Jews' rejection of Christ, and comes out at the end with the conclusion that "all Israel will be saved" (11:26). But on the way he comes up with a number of other answers. Let us see what they are.

1. *Not all "Israelites" are the true Israel* (9:6-8; 11:5-6). Paul falls back on an old doctrine of the prophets, the Remnant. Most of Israel were a bad lot. Isaiah and Amos and the rest of the prophets had no illusions about that. But there was always a remnant of true God-fearers. For Paul, the "remnant" are those who lived by faith, who knew, without the Letter to the

Romans to help them, that the way to God's acceptance is simply to accept his grace as a gift. These are the true Israelites, and they are being saved; they have found the same way of faith that all Christians have found. So there is no problem; for all of the *real Israel* are being saved.

2. *God can do what he pleases, with and to whom he pleases* (9:10-21, 25-29). Man is no more than a piece of clay in a potter's hands. No clay has a right to question what the potter makes of it. God saves some. It is his will to do so. He rejects others. It's not a matter of justice or injustice, only a matter of divine, infinite Power which no human being has any right to question.

3. *God has stood a good deal, and has been patient.* When finally his wrath destroys the "vessels of wrath" (the wicked Jews and Gentiles), his mercy on some will shine all the brighter (9:22-24). This is tied in with the second answer above. There the emphasis is on God's power; here the emphasis is on his mercy. The fact that he is merciful to anyone offsets the destruction which, in this view, is visited on those who well deserve it.

4. *The Jews went their own way; they simply suffer the consequences* (9:30-33). Paul has not forgotten what he said earlier in this letter: to use his own imagery, pursuing the righteousness which is based on Law never succeeds in fulfilling the Law. Most of the Jews persisted in building ladders to heaven made of their own good deeds. Such ladders, so to speak, always break. In other words, the moral laws of the universe have destroyed those who thought that by them they could win the favor of God. As Paul puts it elsewhere (Rom. 14:23), whatever does not proceed from faith is sin.

5. *The Jews have not had their chance yet* (10:1-17). Romans 10:14-15 has been used as a text for missionary sermons time out of mind; but it is often overlooked that the thought here is of missions to the Jews, first of all. The point is that while no one can be saved outside of Christ, one cannot say that the Jews as a whole have rejected him; they have not yet heard of him. (Can Paul here be wishing that God will raise up a more successful evangelist to the Jews than he had been?)

6. *The elect "obtained" salvation; the others (non-elect) "were hardened"* (11:7). This may well be another form of the second answer, without the figure of the potter and the clay. Some are elect—that is to say, chosen—and some are not. It is as simple

as that. On this view, if any Israelite is lost, that is a sign that
God had no intention of saving him. The elect, those whom
God does intend to be saved, will be saved.

7. *The hostility and stubbornness of Israel is a good thing in
the long run, for it is producing and will produce the salvation
of the Gentiles* (11:13-24). It is clear that Paul does not wish
this answer to be taken alone but in connection with the eighth
answer below. At any rate, this thought may have occurred to
him through reflecting on his own experience. Suppose he had
been as successful among the Jews, his own people, as he had
tried to be? He could have had a busy life as a missionary to
Israelites, but in that case who would or could have done what
he had done among the Gentiles? Paul had no false modesty. He
knew what he meant to the Church; he knew what his gifts were.
So he could honestly say that being thrown out of the synagogues
and blockaded away from his own people was really a blessing
in disguise.

8. *All Israel will be saved* (11:1, 2, 26). God has not rejected
them. There is no problem, really, because we are seeing only
what has taken place *so far*. God's *final* intention is to do what
we have hastily wished he would do right now, that is, save all
his people Israel. Indeed, it is better this way; for the delay in the
salvation of Israel is just what is opening the way for the gospel
among the Gentiles. This does not solve the problem for us in
the twentieth century, for it raises this further question: Does
"all Israel" mean all there will be of Israel at some future date
known only to God? Or does it include the millions of Israelites
who have lived and died since A.D. 30? If the former, then not
all Israel will have been saved; if the latter, then how are these
now-dead Israelites to hear the gospel?

Paul's next-to-last word on this problem is on a note of universal hope: "God has consigned all men to disobedience, that
he may have mercy upon all." But his last word is, characteristi-
cally, an outburst of praise to the inscrutable God: "O the depth
of the riches and wisdom and knowledge of God! . . . who has
known the mind of the Lord . . . ? . . . To him be glory forever"
(11:33-36).

Notes on Particular Points

Does Paul call Jesus God? (9:5). The Greek of this verse can
be translated either as the Revised Standard Version has it in the

text, or as it has it in the margin. If the first translation is correct, then he does not, but if the second is correct, then he does identify Christ as the high God. All that can be said is that while the translation given in the margin is quite possible, if it is what Paul means it is quite out of line with his regular way of speaking about Christ. Paul many times has excellent chances to say that Christ is God, but he avoids saying it (see for instance I Cor. 3:23, where instead of saying Christ is God, he says "Christ is God's"—he belongs to God).

In 9:22 Paul says that vessels of wrath are "made for destruction." The potter makes one vessel for beauty and another for menial use. Much later in life Paul uses the same figure of speech but with a different meaning (II Tim. 2:20-21). In Romans 9:22 the vessel of dishonor is not to be changed; in II Timothy a vessel made for "ignoble" use may by purifying himself become a "vessel . . . consecrated and useful."

Paul was a theologian of high rank; the Church has never placed anyone beside him. But he had no theological conceit. He did not confuse theology with faith. God does not think most highly of the people who can pass theological examinations with the highest marks. Paul never says: In order to be saved you must believe every word I have written. He does not say: Either believe as I do or you are no true Christian. In one sentence (10:9) he makes it quite plain that there are two essentials. One is to acknowledge Jesus as Lord; the other is to believe in your heart that God raised him from the dead. Paul does not say that this is all there is to Christian belief. He does say that this much is saving faith. (There is much food for thought here.)

Paul was a city man, and his illustration in 11:17-24 suggests a procedure just backwards from what is actually done in orchards. Wild shoots are not grafted in to cultivated trees, but the other way around. The kind of fruit depends not on the stock but on the grafted-in branches. However, his readers were city people too, and so probably most of them, like most readers of Romans to this day, never noticed this point. Taken not as information about horticulture but as a made-up illustration, it carries Paul's point.

One verse (11:32) has disturbed some people, because it does not seem to be "orthodox." The orthodox view (among all churches that make a point of orthodoxy) is that some people are *not* saved and never will be. The view expressed by this verse is called "universalism" and is widely though not officially held in many churches. Paul himself in other places expresses a different view from universalism, as for instance in II Thessalonians 1:8-9 and Philippians 3:19. It is not of much use to claim that "have mercy" here does not mean "save," for not only does the expression "have mercy" (referring to God) imply salvation, but if it meant anything less here it would spoil the point of the sentence. All this is one reason for supposing that Paul in these chapters is not laying down final answers, but only debating the possibilities.

Many people have understood Romans 9:19-21, indeed all of chapter 9, to teach "double predestination." Many others cannot see that doctrine here. Double predestination is the doctrine, found in a few creeds of Christendom, that God "foreordained" certain persons to everlasting life and others to everlasting death. To foreordain is to render the occurrence of a future event certain. Calvin put it this way: God creates some men for the purpose of salvation, others for the purpose of damnation. Now, not all those who believe in "double predestination" agree with Calvin that God decides even before he creates a human being whether or not he will ever save the person he creates. A more usual supposition is that after mankind had fallen into sin, God decided once for all that he would save certain ones ("election is selection," as one man put it), and in the same act of decision decided not to save all or any of the rest, but to pass them by. This is sometimes called the doctrine of "preterition" or "passing-by." At any rate, both Calvin's doctrine and the doctrine of preterition teach "double predestination"; for in both views not only does God know beforehand who are to be saved, but he knows because he himself has fixed in advance, made absolutely certain and definite, not only the salvation of each saved person but the damnation of every lost one—and this long before they were born.

There is no room to argue the pros and cons of the argument whether double predestination is true. The point is, those who take it in either Calvin's or the other form, believe they find Bible support for their belief in Romans 9. The reader may think they are right, or he may not; he will have company either way. In any case, this commentator would advise caution. For the simple and obvious fact, often overlooked by argumentative theologians, is that Paul in these chapters 9-11 is not discussing individual salvation at all, but the salvation of *Israel*. It is a little risky to use these chapters alone to support any theory about *individual* salvation.

THE PRACTICAL LIVING OF CHRISTIANS
Romans 12:1—15:13

One who is reading Romans for the first time might think the end of chapter 11 a good place to stop. After pursuing this problem of how the Chosen People can possibly be lost, how the "People of the Promise" could miss receiving the promise, after penetrating the problem as far as he can go, Paul breaks out into eloquent yet reverent words of praise to the God of mystery, might—and mercy. He writes "Amen" just as if he were through.

People who have read other letters of Paul's would know he is not through. For he never finishes a letter without coming down to brass tacks, so to speak, getting down to the particulars of living. The good news about God and his free grace, his mercy that is stronger than sin, is not simply something to be listened to. If all we do is listen, it shows we have not heard with our hearts, only with our ears. If we really hear and believe, then after the "Amen" comes a "therefore." Since these things are so, what then for us? Does the life of faith mean that we always stand like beggars with outstretched hands, taking what mercy God gives, striving only to be nothing that he may be all in all? By no means. God's love, his grace, the sacrifice of Christ, we have to take with simple humility and thankfulness. It is "bestowed" on us, not produced by us. But Paul has already in chapters 5-8 insisted that justification, the pardoning mercy of God, does not stand alone; it has results in life and the Christian is challenged and commanded to live accordingly. If the reader will glance back at those chapters he will see that the Christian life there is expressed in very general terms, sometimes even mystical: as, for instance, "We rejoice in our sufferings, knowing that suffering produces . . . character" (5:3-4); "walk in newness of life" (6:4); "consider yourselves dead to sin and alive to God" (6:11); you "have become slaves of righteousness" (6:18); "yield your members to righteousness for sanctification" (6:19).

Paul now in chapter 12 goes on into particulars. What does all this high language about newness of life, sanctification, and so on,

mean in the practical situations of life? Paul had never
seen that church in Rome. Its members had not asked him any
questions, or brought him any problems to solve. But he knew
that in Rome Christians met the same essential problems which
they meet everywhere. That is one reason this chapter 12 appeals
so strongly to all Christians; just because it is general it speaks
to all sorts and conditions of men.

A Note on Status and State

This is a good place to stop and think about the difference
between justification and sanctification, and how they are related.
In shorter words we can call it the difference between *status* and
state, in the Christian life. A simple illustration will make this
clear. Suppose a mother hears the front door bell ring, and when
she answers it sees her six-year-old Willie—covered with mud,
maybe with a small turtle in his hand. The mother does not invite the child in, she gives him a lecture. "Don't you bring that
turtle into the house," she says, "and don't put your foot inside
this clean front door. Go around to the back and leave your
clothes on the porch and go right upstairs to the bathroom and
wait till I come up and give you a scrubbing."

Now that boy's *status,* that is to say his *standing,* with his
mother could not be better. He is her son. She has no intention
of disowning him; indeed, she loves him dearly. But his *state*
is deplorable. He is dirty as homemade sin; he is not fit to associate with the family. But because of his status, his mother is concerned with his state. A neighbor's child could be just as dirty and
she would do nothing about it. But because Willie is her boy she
not only does not like the state he is in, but she does something
about it. Let a salesman come to the door in the best possible state
—suit pressed, shirt spotless, shaved, and scrubbed to a sanitary
polish; she will not let him in front door or back. His state may
be good but his status is not.

Now justification is the word we use—taking it from Paul—for
the Christian's status with God. Sanctification is the word—again
from Paul but not exclusive with him—for our state. *Status* we
can only accept, as children accept their parents and their parents' love. But *state* we can and must do something about. Just as
the initiative, the suggestion, the push, for that little boy's bath
has to come from his mother, so the initiative for a cleaner state

of the Christian's life comes from God. Yet the little boy is expected to co-operate, and so are we with God.

What has just been said is in line, we believe, with the teaching of the New Testament and with Paul in particular. Yet there are three other views which have been held. One is that our state is something God alone produces: sanctification is a work of the Holy Spirit exclusively. An opposite view is that we alone are responsible for the state we are in, we are responsible for our own spiritual and moral growth: sanctification is the Christian's work exclusively. A third view is that justification and sanctification are both divine make-believes; that justification is God saying, "Not guilty," when we really are guilty, and sanctification is God saying, "Better and better," when we are really growing no better at all. The reader may check all these views with Paul's teaching.

There is a sense in which, all scholars agree, the Greek words usually translated "holy" and "holiness" refer to consecration or dedication. In this sense, sanctification or dedication is a *status* as well as a *state*. But there is also a use of the word "holy" and "holiness" or "sanctification" to mean a state, condition, or process, in which both God and man are active (see, for example, Rom. 6:19; I Cor. 6:11; II Cor. 1:12; 7:1; Eph. 1:4; 5:26-27; I Thess. 4:3; 5:23).

If sanctification were God's work alone, we should be no more than mechanical dolls manufactured and wound up by God. If sanctification were all our own work, then we would not need God in our lives at all. All Christian experience cries "No!" to such thoughts. If sanctification were no more than a legal fiction, then the whole New Testament would no longer make sense. For the New Testament is more than sprinkled with imperatives, commands, directives. Surely these are not intended to make Christian goodness nothing better than a pure pretense!

The Principle of the Christian Life (12:1-2)

Paul has already written, as we have seen, about the Christian life. But now in chapters 12-14 he brings all he has said into focus. This is not a sort of appendix to the letter, it is a necessary part of it. Christian *living* is no take-it-or-leave-it extra, it is welded to the gospel. Paul never preached the gospel without speaking of Christian living, and no one can claim to believe the gospel while leaving Christian living on one side.

Paul puts something new into the idea of sacrifice. The Old Testament sacrifices were always something the sacrificer *possessed*. Now Paul emphasizes sacrificing *oneself*. Furthermore, certain sacrifices involved total destruction, or at least the removal of the thing sacrificed from the use of man. Nobody *ate* a burnt offering, neither God nor man. What was left of the sin offering was never returned to the one who gave it. The one type of ancient sacrifice which was shared by the offerer was the peace offering, something that could be as gay as a church picnic.

True, some of the prophets saw a higher kind of sacrifice, the "broken and contrite heart" (Ps. 51:16-17; Micah 6:8). These insights were rare, but they lie behind Paul's radical ideal. The Christians had no altars, and doubtless were criticized by their pagan neighbors for not having them. The Christian's sacrifice to God is not something that he has; it is rather all that he *is*. Christian sacrifice is not destruction, it is service; it is being-used. Old-time sacrifice was the offer of something less than oneself, to be removed from use. The new sacrifice required of Christians is nothing less than oneself, made fit for use, and used.

Note several points here about the Christian life. First, its motive is gratitude for God's love in Christ, the "mercies" of God. It is not that Paul throws good works down the front steps in chapter 4 and brings them in by the back door in chapter 12. What Paul has thrown out is the idea that by good works we can *earn* the mercy of God. What he brings in is that by good works we express our *gratitude* to God who makes it possible for us even to wish to do anything good, and, much more, who gives us power to do it.

Second, the Christian life is not simply a "spiritual" one. If we are not Christian *in* and *with* our bodies, we are not Christian. Paul *begins* with the body, in fact. Why not "present your *souls* a living sacrifice"? Because unless the body is consecrated, it is not realistic to talk about "spiritual" consecration. One easy way to hypocrisy is to think that if your soul is holy ("if your heart is in the right place") what you do with your body makes no difference. The Bible, taken seriously, keeps man from thinking he is an angel. Angels are pure spirits; man is body and spirit one and inseparable.

Third, Christian life begins in the mind. Paul means more than intellect here; he means the whole inner life of man. But he uses the word which more than any other points to man the thinker.

The transformation of the mind is the base of the process of growing as a Christian. This reminds us of Jesus, who strongly preached repentance. For repentance means precisely this making over, this reorientation of the mind.

Fourth, the Christian life is one which follows the will of God, and this will can be identified in certain ways. To be sure, we can be mistaken about what the will of God is; but we can hardly be mistaken about what that will is *not*. If something about which we are in doubt is not good, not acceptable (in line with what we do know of God's will in general), and not perfect (or as near perfection as the situation permits), then it cannot confidently be called God's will.

The Practice of the Christian Life (12:3—15:13)

Individual Christian Living (12:3-21)

What Paul says in detail about the Christian life is so clear, simple, and helpful that a commentator only gets in the way if he tries to gild the lily by making further remarks.

Christians and Government (13:1-7)

This chapter has puzzled people who know their Roman history. The emperor at this time was Nero, the infamous Nero, the same one who later fiddled while Rome burned, the cruel brute who had evening parties in gardens where light was furnished by the flames of living human bodies smeared with pitch and burned. How could Paul call such a man an "authority . . . from God," a "terror to bad conduct"?

One way to solve the difficulty is to take all this not as referring to one particular emperor, but to the Empire as such. Paul felt that the Empire was (unintentionally, no doubt) the most powerful friend the Church had. It kept the peace far and wide; and missionaries went where they pleased, many of them protected, as Paul was, by the Roman laws. Another solution is to say that Paul was supporting the Empire in opposition to the numerous anti-government "underground" organizations, run by Jewish extremists. The Jews were a notoriously riotous people, and Paul did not wish the Christians, a very new sect as the Romans would see it, to be identified as subversive or on the government's black list.

Still another suggestion is that although some Christians were already thinking of the Roman Empire as Antichrist, Paul thought of it as the power that held Antichrist back. On this view, II Thessalonians 2:6-7 refers to the Roman Empire. If this is the case, then of course Paul would regard the Empire as God's appointed servant.

Another and simpler explanation is that at the time Paul wrote this letter, Nero was in the "honeymoon" of his reign; the Empire generally was well governed, and Nero himself had not developed the extreme cruelty and insanity which ruined his later years.

Christians down the ages have disagreed over this chapter. By those who take it literally and apply the words to *all* governments, this chapter has been used to bolster the *status quo,* the existing government no matter how bad, inefficient, or cruel.

In the twentieth century this has been an agonizing problem for Christians in many lands. When the Nazis took over Germany, many Christians on the outside wondered why Christians did not protest more than they did against the cruelties planned and practiced by Hitler's hoodlums. But in the German churches the people had had it drilled into them for centuries: Church and State are separate realms. The Church has no right to criticize the State; "he who resists the authorities resists what God has appointed" (13:2). It was only when the State began to interfere with the Church that Christians woke up. Today, people in Western countries often forget that on the other side of the Iron Curtain are millions of Christians. What are they to do under an atheistic, antireligious government? At what point must a Christian citizen turn rebel?

Two points seem clear, though how to apply them has to be left to the judgment of those who are caught in the dilemma. First, patriotic support of one's own government is a part of the Christian's duty. In our democratic era we can often say that a Christian's duty is *participation in* government; this in Paul's time was clearly impossible. Second, government is an authority from God only so far as, and as long as, it fits the description Paul gives of it. Indeed, this passage from Romans is a sort of handy indicator by which to tell good government from bad. Does the government, local or national as the case may be, in fact encourage good people and discourage bad ones? Is it the kind of government free Christians can respect? If not, and if its ills are incurable, then surely it can no longer claim to be "from God."

This passage about government illustrates also another point:
that specific teaching in the Bible about specific problems cannot
always be used as simply as a lobster fisherman uses his brass
gadget to measure whether a lobster is of legal size or not. Moral
problems even for Christians cannot be settled by brass rulers.
For example: about the year 1860 a very conscientious Christian
named Robert E. Lee was faced with a choice between loyalty to
the United States of America and to his home state. The American Civil War was about to begin. Lee was offered the position
of top general of all the United States armies. Should he be loyal
to the country in whose army he had long served, or to the state
where he was born? Colonel Lee could not settle that problem
simply by reading Romans 13:1-7. The Bible is not a rulebook
covering all cases. Not even for the most conscientious Christian
will the Bible save him the trouble of *thinking,* or guarantee that
his interpretation will be always right.

Love and the Law (13:8-10)

Anyone who thinks Paul a legalist, a cold theologian, surely
must have stopped reading Romans long before reaching chapter
13. Here we meet law again, *the* Law, too, of which Paul had
said that the only good it did was to stir up a perverse desire to
violate it. But now Paul tells us that *love* "is the fulfilling of the
law." There is no contradiction really between what he says here
and what he said, for example, in chapters 4 and 7. There, he was
speaking of the Law as a code *outside me,* a set of Thou-shalt's,
Thou-shalt-not's, thrown at me, my constant accuser, my final
despair. Here, Paul is speaking of the Law *within me* (see Jer.
31:33), not as a set of rules but as the expression of love. Love
is not a sentiment or an emotion; in the New Testament sense—
in the sense in which Paul himself elsewhere describes it (I Cor.
13)—it is a continuing steady concern for the good of others not
less than oneself. Love is the very basis of justice; love that is
lawless is not God-like. Law and justice not rooted in love can be
the most cruel injustice.

Make No Room for Evil (13:11-14)

Practically everybody who writes a book on Romans has to
tell the famous story connected with these verses, especially with
verse 14. Since presumably many readers of this present book
have not yet heard the story, here it is again. A young man of

great wealth who later became famous was convinced in his mind
that Christianity was right and true, but in his heart and will he
could not break away from his sin. He was a much torn and distressed man. One day in a garden, where he had been reading this
same Letter to the Romans, he heard children's voices from over
the wall, *"Tolle, lege; tolle, lege."* That was in the days when
many people spoke Latin. The words he heard could mean two
things. One was, "Put, take." Probably some little girls were playing a game of some kind. But the words also mean, "Take, read."
It was like an angel's voice to him. So he took the book, and
there leaped out to his eye Romans 13:14. He read no further.
"At the end of that sentence," he wrote afterwards, "all the shades
of doubt were scattered." That was the moment when Augustine,
later Bishop of Hippo, Saint of the Church universal, and one of
the most influential minds in the past 2000 years, became a Christian.

But also for those who are already Christians (as were those to
whom Paul was actually writing) this is one of the great sentences
of Scripture. When sins shake us that we should have shaken off,
why is it? Is it not because we have made the way ready for the
sin? We do nothing to prevent it beforehand. Put into very simple
English, Paul is saying: Do not plan for sin; give it no welcome;
offer it no opportunity. Kick the sin off your doorstep and you
won't have it in the house.

The Strong and the Weak (14:1—15:13)

Paul now comes to something which is a problem always and
everywhere: *moral questions about which sincere Christians differ.*
Just because Christian life cannot be managed with a brass rule,
just because a slogan like "Love is the answer" or "Christ is the
answer" does not untangle all problems, the Christian often has
to think his problems through—only to find that other equally
sincere Christians have thought the same problems through and
have come up with quite different answers. Then what?

Paul mentions two such problems. We can pass by the first,
the question of whether or not to observe certain special religious
days (was one of them the Sabbath?), as Paul says little about
it and what little he says is clear. The other question was a very
thorny one. We find him dealing with it in the Corinthian church
(I Cor. 8). It had to do with eating meat. For some Christians
today that is a religious question, but it was a different kind of

religious question in the Roman Empire. The fact is, in a Roman market you could hardly find a steak or a roast or any kind of meat that had not come from some animal slaughtered in a heathen temple. The animal would be killed as a sacrifice; then the priests (who, numerous though they were, could not possibly eat all the animals the people offered) would sell the meat through retail outlets. This being the major source of meats on the market, the Christian shopper was faced with a problem: in buying and eating this meat, am I or am I not helping out the heathen worship? Is not my witness for Christ better shown by simply not eating meat at all? Some Christians answered both questions "Yes," and so would not eat any meat. Others said that meat was meat—it was *people* who were heathen, not beefsteaks.

Paul assumes that both sides are right, *from their own point of view* (14:14). Then which viewpoint is right? Paul is personally sure that the more liberal point of view is the right one. Nothing is unclean (unfit for a Christian to eat) in itself. It is quite true that a steak is only a steak; there are no steaks infected with heresy! The "strong" man, the man with the broader view, might ask Paul: Am I right? Paul would say, Yes. The man might ask, What harm can come to me if I eat such meat? Paul would say, No harm whatever. Is it a sin? Not even a tiny one.

But Paul lifts the question clear out of the self-centered level of what *I* think, what's good for *me,* and sets it on a different level altogether, the high level of *love.* What will your action do to this weaker man? Remember he is your brother. Suppose he follows your example, as he is very likely to do? Then he will be *going against his conscience,* and that will cause his "ruin" (vs. 15). If the "strong man" complains that this ties down his freedom, Paul reminds him that Christ did more than give up freedom —*Christ died for him.*

The reader will find much more in this section, but this is the main point. (The word "faith" in 14:23 clearly has a different meaning from what it had in earlier chapters. Here it means conviction or assurance.) The chain of quotations in chapter 15:1-13 and the prayers in that chapter are along this same line of raising a moral problem out of the rulebook and looking at it in the light of the divine love. No human problem has been seen right until it has been seen in the light of God. No human problem can be wisely approached and solved apart from applying the principle of love. There will always be differing opinions, but they should not mar the harmony Christians enjoy "with one another, in accord with Christ Jesus" (15:5).

PERSONAL NOTES AND BENEDICTION
Romans 15:14—16:27

Where Did Romans Originally End?

Ancient Greek handwritten copies of this letter, still in existence, do not agree about the arrangement of the doxology now found at the very end. That is, of course, the best place for it; but the majority of old copies have it at the end of chapter 14. One has it after 15, some have it twice—once after 14, once after 16—and a few leave it out entirely. Add to this the fact that the earliest "table of contents" we have (in Latin) of Paul's letters, omits chapters 15 and 16 entirely. All this has led most scholars to agree that this Letter to the Romans circulated in two or three editions, as we would say; one ended with chapter 14, one with 16, and (perhaps) one with 15. Without going into the discussion, it seems likely that Paul wrote the letter as we have it, and that someone (perhaps Paul himself?) who wanted to circulate the letter among other churches, cut off these last two chapters because they were personal to the Romans.

We have mentioned this not because it is very important in itself either way, but to illustrate a kind of problem which has no absolutely certain answer and yet does not affect anything fundamental. There are many variations in the thousands of Greek manuscripts of the New Testament, and it is seldom possible to say with one hundred per cent certainty, for half a page together, what the *original* copy contained. And yet in all these variant readings, as they are technically called, there are no differences so great as to affect a single Christian doctrine in a serious way.

Hopes, Prayers, and Realities (15:14-33)

Paul has hardly been personal since chapter 1, but now the man himself speaks some final words about himself, his plans, and the Roman Christians. Again we reach a section which mostly speaks for itself, without needing a commentary. Paul emphasizes his place as "minister of Christ Jesus to the Gentiles" as if the Roman church were all Gentile. He speaks of his ambition to be a missionary in the pioneering sense, preaching to people who never heard so much as the name of Christ. His plan for his next months and years sounded far more daring—and was—than a similar travel plan would sound today. Remember he was in Corinth when he wrote. His next main destination was Jerusalem, then Rome, then Spain. Jerusalem and Rome of course were not virgin territory for Christianity or for Paul. But he had special reasons for visiting each: Jerusalem first, because for some time Paul had been gathering an offering of money from the churches of Asia, to send to the now poor and hungry Christians in the mother-city of Judea. It was typical of Paul to wish to go to Jerusalem personally with this gift. We read more about it in Second Corinthians. The point here is that Paul was so intent on taking this gift personally that he entirely overlooked the grave danger of such a trip. It was as much as his life was worth to go to Jerusalem; his enemies there were more numerous, more bitter than anywhere else.

Then he was going to Rome, not to "evangelize" the city—others were doing that—but to be "refreshed in your company" (15:32). Perhaps he was intending to make Rome the base of his future operations. Paul was not a rich man. To travel and work as far away as Spain would cost money, and Paul had no missionary society to supply what he needed. He may have hoped that Roman Christians would be that society, at least for his work. He had made it plain enough in this letter that the whole Church should be missionary. A church that is not missionary-minded is hardly a true church. But particular projects need particular sponsors, and Paul evidently was "cultivating" the interest of Roman Christians in the far horizons. Spain, though about as far away as a man could travel in the Roman Empire, was still a vigorous part of the Empire. Some of the most distinguished persons in Roman life at that time were from Spain.

Jerusalem—Rome—Spain. As travel was then, it was like saying, "Moscow—Johannesburg—Spitzbergen." Only a wide-horizoned man, and a brave one, could have had such a hope.

Personal Greetings (16:1-23)

As we said earlier, some people have been inclined to believe that this chapter must originally have been a part of some other letter to another church. How could Paul know so many people in a church he had never visited? However, the best of the old Greek copies contain this chapter, and it is not at all impossible that Paul had known these people elsewhere. Which of us does not know friends who have moved to great cities far away? The reader is invited not to skim these names but to read the list with care. A good deal about Paul himself comes out here. This is no pompous religious professional, no cold scholar interested only in professors, but a true man who treasures every friend he makes.

To God Be the Glory (16:25-27)

This long letter ends with a Hallelujah, a doxology of praise to God. If we did not have other letters from Paul's later life, we might wonder whether as an old man, ill and poor and in jail, he would not suffer from disappointment and disillusionment, and end his days in a different spirit from this. For the hopes and prayers of this letter were not all to be fulfilled. He did reach Jerusalem, but from that point on nothing went according to plan—his plan, that is. He was nearly assassinated there, and was never a free man again, except perhaps for a short time near the end of his life. He did reach Rome, but not in triumph. He came to that city in chains, a prisoner. So far as the New Testament tells us, he never set eyes on Spain.

Nevertheless, feeble and old, with prospects for his future dim and grim, he never lost the sense of the grace of the Lord Jesus and the glory of God. He lived the life he commended, bearing witness, by his own life of faith and triumphant joy, to the truth of what he taught. Through the centuries his witness has been multiplied beyond counting, as Christians around the world have rediscovered with Paul the measureless glory and the overflowing grace of God in Christ.

THE FIRST LETTER OF PAUL TO THE

CORINTHIANS

INTRODUCTION

Paul, the Author

Paul is so well known that no biography of him, not even a thumbnail sketch, will be given here. The basic facts about him are in the Book of Acts, and in his own letters. How these are put together, along with some side information drawn from history outside the Bible, the reader may read for himself in a good Bible dictionary.

What we need to remember about Paul, in connection with these Corinthian letters, is that he had a good reason to know the Corinthian church, its members and its problems. He had founded the church himself, from nothing at all, for so far as we know there were no Christians in that city when Paul arrived. Unlike Romans, which was written mostly to strangers, in a strange church in a strange city, these letters were written to personal friends, in a situation Paul knew very well.

Paul and the Church at Corinth

Any man who had the intention of telling the story of Jesus in the Roman Empire would certainly have Corinth on his itinerary, though Paul's actual going there might seem to have been almost an accident. He had been in different places in Macedonia, to the north, but had been driven out by rioters. "Wherever Paul went," it has been said, "there was either a revival or a riot." And sometimes both! He then went to Athens, where he had a short and not entirely successful stay. From there he went to Corinth "in weakness and in much fear and trembling," as he himself said (I Cor. 2:3). After being driven out of Thessalonica and Beroea, and after what must have been a disheartening experience in Athens, no wonder he was not filled with confidence at the sight of Corinth. It was like Chicago, "stormy, husky, brawling." It needed Christianity; but would this city take it? At first the answer seemed to be, No. Paul began his work, as always if possible, by speaking in the local synagogue. As a rabbi from the beloved capital of all Jewish people, and (as is probable) a former member of the High Court or Sanhedrin there, Paul would be welcome in any synagogue, and sooner or later would be asked for "a few remarks." One thing led to another, and presently Paul was speaking every Sabbath (Saturday) in the synagogue, and winning converts too. This led to a riot, but Paul was not to be stopped. He announced that he now would go to the Gentiles, then he moved next door and started a church in the house of Titius Justus, presumably a Roman.

For eighteen months Paul stayed there, talking to anyone who would listen, teaching, counseling, quietly gathering a Christian church. As to what the church was like, First Corinthians gives us the inside information. At all events, after eighteen months there was another riot. Paul took his time about leaving, but "after . . . many days" set off for Jerusalem and Antioch. He stayed in Corinth longer than any other city on his travels, except Ephesus where on a later visit he remained about three years.

The Corinthian Correspondence

While Paul was in Ephesus, two or three years after this, he had occasion to write the Corinthians a letter, which he mentions in I Corinithians 5:9. It is possible, and even probable, that II Corinthians 6:14—7:1 is a quotation from that letter. At any rate, that passage represents the spirit of the letter to which Paul refers in I Corinthians 5:9.

Sometime after this, Paul heard of troubles in the church at Corinth. Besides, the members of the church wrote him a letter asking his advice on a variety of problems they had. In answer to that letter, Paul wrote what we know as First Corinthians. Unfortunately the letter did not produce good results. Paul himself had to leave Ephesus and pay the Corinthians a visit—not a pleasant one. He was in the position of a minister with a church that asks his advice but has no intention of taking it. (Some scholars believe Paul made the trip to Corinth from some other city than Ephesus, but the point does not seem to be important, either way.)

So Paul, after reaching Ephesus again, sent the Corinthians a scorching letter to which he himself refers in II Corinthians 2:4

and II Corinthians 7:8. Indeed, Paul admits that he almost regrets that he wrote such a letter at all. This severe letter worked, however; and so Paul writes still another letter, which is (see below) either all or a part of our Second Corinthians.

Is that "severe letter" in existence? Many interpreters have given convincing arguments that we do have at least a large part of that severe letter, in II Corinthians 10-13. Whoever thought first of publishing Paul's letters would likely write around to churches where he was known to have worked, to see if he had written them any letters. The Corinthian church would presumably go through their files (as we say) and send all they thought wise to release to the Church at large. The collectors or editors would then in all probability combine two or three letters, or parts of letters, though not in the original order. That may or may not have been the case with the Corinthian correspondence. At any rate, Second Corinthians seems to make more sense if we think of chapters 10-13 as the severe letter, or most of it; and chapters 1-9 as the letter of reconciliation. (More about that when we come to it.)

In this theory the whole correspondence would be something like this:

1. Paul's first letter (either now lost, or else a fragment of it preserved in II Cor. 6:14—7:1).

2. The Corinthians' letter to Paul (referred to in I Cor. 7:1), now lost.

3. First Corinthians, written by Paul in answer to their letter to him.

4. The severe letter, referred to in II Corinthians 2:4 and 7:8. Probably preserved in II Corinthians 10-13.

5. The "letter of reconciliation," the cheerful and relaxed chapters 1-9 of Second Corinthians.

The City of Corinth

Much in these letters can be better understood by knowing something about the city of Corinth. Just as churches today in different countries or even in different sections of the same city reflect the kind of places where they are, so in Corinth. It was a big city and the church was very small. You would have had a harder time finding the church there than you have finding, say, Christadelphians in New York without the help of newspaper ads or phone book.

Corinth was a new city, comparatively speaking. It had been burned to the ground by a Roman general's orders back in 146 B.C., lay in ashes for one hundred years, and then got a new start. Like all new cities "zoned commercial" it had few "fine old traditions." Everybody was out for the almighty drachma. It was a great shipping port. All the cargoes going east or west across the Isthmus of Corinth were handled at Corinth city. The Isthmian Games, a big athletic series, were held near there. The general morals of the place were even lower than the average of cities in the Roman Empire, so much so that the word "Corinthianize" was used to refer to unmentionable sins.

The city was at the same time a very tough place to start a church, and a wonderful place too. It was tough because while the place reeked with "religions," some of them were so depraved that even the Roman government refused to license them. The people were mostly hard-boiled lovers of pleasure, materialists to the core, the last people in the world you would think capable of "spiritual" understanding or living. If you could get a church going in Corinth, you could get it going anywhere. That little church at Corinth was a real experiment station. It was demonstrated there once and for all that the Christian faith can take root anywhere. After Corinth, you cannot point to any part of the world, then or since, and say, "That place is so degraded that it is useless to send Christian workers there."

Corinth was a great place to begin a church for another reason. Just because it was a kind of Chicago of its time, a center of trade and transportation, a big business city and sports center also, anything well started in Corinth would soon make its way to other parts of the Empire. Paul was himself a city man and he knew the importance of the city. He never visited villages. This was not because he thought villagers not worth saving, but villagers in those days died where they were born and lived. It was the city people who traveled; it was city Christians who would carry the gospel out on highways and seaways to the frontiers of the Empire and beyond.

Date and Authorship of Corinthians

In this commentary, where the whole Corinthian correspondence is meant the one word "Corinthians" includes it all. Where the reference is to just one of these letters, the numbers I and II will be used.

Placing the activities and the letters of Paul in their right years in history is a kind of jigsaw puzzle. If you are curious enough, you may find a variety of answers in various books. One thing is certain; the Corinthian Letters were earlier than the Letter to Rome by two or three years, since they were written while Paul was headquartered in Ephesus, and Romans was written after Paul had left that city. If we set the date of A.D. 55 for Corinthians and A.D. 58 for Romans, we shall not be far wrong.

There is no doubt that Paul wrote these letters. Doubts have been expressed about a few of the letters attributed to Paul, but not about these. This fact is important, because when you read Corinthians, you are reading unquestionably firsthand materials, written by a man who was in the midst of what he was writing about. Romans may have been written with half an eye to circulating it among other churches; but the Corinthian Letters were written to a particular church about its particular problems, with no apparent thought of publication.

A Note on Paul's Style

Four points should be remembered when reading Paul's writings.

1. He did not actually write his letters himself; they were dictated (see Romans 16:22, for example). There is some reason to believe that Paul's eyesight was very poor, and he may not even have read them over. So we do not have the style of a man sitting at a desk writing, crossing out, erasing, writing again, looking at his outline to make sure of not going off on tangents. It is the style of a man sometimes thinking while he talks, and sometimes putting into a rush of words something he has had on his mind for a long time. It is the style of a man who as preacher and teacher knew the value of repeating an idea, even a word, over and over until it sticks. It is the style of a man with a very lively, "that-reminds-me" sort of mind. He will go off the highway of his main idea into a detour, and then off on a detour from the detour, just as people do when they are talking. Hence Paul is the despair of tidy minds, and it is impossible to make perfect outlines of writing that did not have a clear outline to begin with.

2. Paul lacked three things no present-day theologian would

do without. One was a copy of a reference Bible. His quotations from the Old Testament are numerous, but seldom word for word. Commentators are not always sure just where the quotations come from. Books were extremely expensive in those days, and Paul was not a rich man. A papyrus copy of the Old Testament, complete, would cost about eight times what a skilled workman, such as Paul was, could earn in a year. This is probably the reason why his Bible quotations seem to be mostly from memory, and are often inaccurate. He knew Hebrew well, and also Greek; so his quotations are sometimes more like the Old Testament Hebrew, although normally they reflect the great Greek translation (the Septuagint) which was to be the standard version used by the Church for three hundred years and more.

3. Another thing Paul lacked was carbon copies of other letters he had written. Some modern commentators are distressed to find that Paul does not always agree with himself at every point. But Paul did not have the advantage the commentator has, of a handy volume of Paul's letters—past and future! We should be thankful for Paul's freedom, not apologetic about it.

4. The third thing he lacked was a copy of the Church's creed. No creed had yet come into existence, not even the Apostles' Creed, still less the Nicene Creed or the Westminster Confession of Faith or the Thirty-nine Articles. Paul was not, strictly speaking, a "systematic theologian." He was a great theological thinker writing letters about pressing problems. But he was never trying to be "orthodox." The great creeds try to agree with Paul, not the other way around. The very fact that Christians of every variety cherish Paul's writings and live by them is evidence enough that his letters cannot be squeezed into the shape of any particular denominational creed. If we find him saying things that do not quite fit the creed of our own church, it is always possible to try to revise his remarks, or to reinterpret them, so that they do fit. But it is more honest to let him say what he does say, and maybe reflect that perhaps our orthodoxy might be wrong at that point!

OUTLINE

Introduction, Blessing and Thanksgiving. I Corinthians 1:1-9

Unity in the Congregation. I Corinthians 1:10—4:21
  The Parties, the Partisans (1:10-17)
  The Key to Unity: the Message of the Cross (1:18—3:4)
  God's Workmen, the Apostles; God's Workmanship, the Church (3:5—4:21)

Immorality of Church Members; Lawsuits Among Christians; Church Discipline. I Corinthians 5:1—6:20

Sex and Marriage. I Corinthians 7:1-40

Food from Idols' Temples: Can Harmless Acts Be Wrong? I Corinthians 8:1—11:1
  The First Answer (8:1-6)
  A Second Answer (8:7-13)
  Paul's Good Example (9:1-27)
  A Bad Example from Ancient Israel (10:1-13)
  Summing Up (10:14—11:1)

Public Worship: Bad and Good Ways. I Corinthians 11:2-34
  Women's Place in the Church (11:2-16)
  Disunity (11:17-22)
  The Lord's Supper (11:23-34)

Spiritual Gifts; Worship (continued). I Corinthians 12:1—14:39
  Spiritual Gifts (12:1-11)
  The Unity of the Church as the Body of Christ (12:12-30)
  The "More Excellent Way" of Love (12:31—13:13)
  The Gift of "Tongues"; a Primitive Worship Service (14:1-40)

The Resurrection and the Life Everlasting. I Corinthians 15:1-58
  The Resurrection of Christ Is a Part of the Gospel (15:1-11)
  Christ's Resurrection and the General Resurrection (15:12-19)
  Adam and Death; Christ and Life (15:20-23)
  The End: God Will Be All in All (15:24-28)
  An Argument from Baptizing for the Dead (15:29-34)
  Faith's Answer to a Foolish Question (15:35-57)
  Imperishable Lives in a Perishing World (15:58)

Closing Notes, Greetings, Benediction. I Corinthians 16:1-24

COMMENTARY

INTRODUCTION, BLESSING AND THANKSGIVING

I Corinthians 1:1-9

Out of the thirteen letters usually attributed to Paul, nine of them begin much as this one does. Paul follows standard practice of his time by opening his letter with his signature, so to speak, and after identifying himself, going on to give high compliments to his readers.

Paul's introductions, however, always have a definitely Christian tone, and he identifies himself these nine times as "an apostle" by the will of God. Paul had thought a great deal about what it meant to be an apostle, and in Corinthians he will go into some detail about it.

Who is this Sosthenes who is named as co-writer of this letter? We know there was a Sosthenes in Corinth who was "ruler of the synagogue" when Paul was there the first time (Acts 18:17), and presumably no friend of Paul's. Had he been converted, and is this the same man? No one knows. One wonders what part this Sosthenes, whoever he was, played in the writing of this letter.

The letter, then, comes from an apostle of Christ and his friend Sosthenes to the "church of God" in Corinth. Incidentally, Paul reminds the Corinthians that they are not alone; there are also those "in every place" who call on the name of (worship) the same Lord.

In fact, we can pick up here three expressions which tell us something about what the Church is. (1) It is made up of "those sanctified in Christ Jesus." The reader will soon see that Paul did not mean to say "sinless." The Greek word means "set apart," "consecrated," "devoted." The Church consists of those who have been dedicated to Christ. (2) Almost the same idea is in the phrase "called to be saints." This word "called" is a significant one in Paul's thought. It is his favorite word for the start of the Christian life. He means called not by some preacher but by the Spirit of God. The Church is composed of those whom God himself has called by name, God's invited guests. God calls them *to be* sanctified, to be saints. The Church is composed of saints-in-the-making, not of finished saints. (3) The Church is also the company of those everywhere who "call on the name of"—that is to say, worship—the Lord Jesus.

Notice that here, as in Romans and elsewhere, Paul associates Jesus Christ with God our Father as the source and giver of grace and peace.

The high praise that Paul gives these Corinthians does not fit them realistically, as the letter promptly shows. It is typical of most of Paul's letters (Galatians being the one exception); yet it is not flattery. Paul looks at his people through bifocal glasses. With one lens he sees them as they are; with the other he sees them as they can become by the grace of God. How can people who have the grace of God in their lives, who are "enriched . . . with . . . all knowledge . . . not lacking in any spiritual gift" —how can they commit the sins and blunders for which Paul proceeds to lay on them the lash of his condemnation? Either the writer is guilty of a glaring contradiction; or the "sins" he mentions are not really sins when committed by people who have all knowledge and all spiritual gifts; or he does not mean to be taken literally when he talks of that knowledge and those gifts. Paul was too clear a thinker to make such an obvious contradiction, and he was too sensitive about right and wrong to suppose (as some did then and have done since) that if a person is just "spiritual" enough, he cannot commit sin. So the best way to take this (and similar passages in most of his letters) is what was just now suggested: those high phrases point to what the intention of God is for these people, what they are called to be and become, rather than what they literally are at the present moment. Whatever we may think about this, Paul had no doubt that his Corinthian friends *had* received the grace of God, and he was grateful.

There is much here, as all through this letter, which cannot be noted for lack of space, but the thoughtful reader is invited to linger and meditate. For example, in verses 2-9, how many ways Paul has of describing the Christian life!

One point needs to be mentioned which comes up later on, and explains some difficulties we shall meet. The "revealing of our Lord Jesus Christ" means what today is called the "Second Coming" of Christ. There is no question that Paul, at the time he wrote this letter, was expecting it at any time. His converts at

Corinth were waiting "for the revealing"—in other words, they were looking for the Second Coming in their own time. Much of what Paul writes, especially on practical problems, stands on that underlying expectation of the soon-coming end of the Old Age and the beginning of the New.

UNITY IN THE CONGREGATION (FIRST OF A SERIES OF PROBLEMS)

I Corinthians 1:10—4:21

The Parties, the Partisans (1:10-17)

The first problem with which Paul deals is one which was left out of the letter to him. He has heard it only through "Chloe's people." These are supposed to have been employees or slaves of Chloe, a wealthy woman of the Corinthian' church. The story they brought was no rumor; there would have been no point in spreading a falsehood, for Paul was sure to find out the truth. The trouble was that the little church in Corinth was split three ways, and maybe four. There was no good reason for it, but the split was a fact. The parties named themselves for the different leaders they knew: Paul and Apollos and Cephas (the native name of Simon Peter). Actually these leaders had no sort of quarrel among themselves. True, they were quite different types, possibly not entirely congenial personally, for we never find them long together. Paul's was the vigorous, restless, lawyer-type mind; he was a real "brain" devoted to the service of Christ. Apollos was an eloquent and rather philosophical kind of man, the sort that made a popular preacher then as now. Peter was the only one of the three who had actually lived with Jesus of Nazareth for three years, and of course that would make him the favorite of many people. He made no pretensions of being a "brain," but had great qualities of leadership. Very likely the Jewish members of the congregation would consider him the Number One leader.

It is likely that there was a fourth party, the "Christ party" as they called themselves. Just as has often happened in Church history since that time, someone starts a church which is a protest against all denominations, but it turns out to be only another denomination after all.

We cannot follow all the ins and outs of Paul's treatment of this problem, but only the main lines of his approach to it. One thing should be said at the very beginning: *Paul never solves any problem in a trivial way*. He brings all problems into the light of God's grace—which is a light that penetrates beneath the surface. If he had gone at the Corinthian church in a superficial sort of way, his letters would hardly have been treasured. But whether or not we have the same problems today (some we have with us yet, some not), what helps us is not so much the particular answer Paul arrives at for Corinth in the year A.D. 55, as the methods and principles he uses, which are good for our problems in the twentieth century or any time.

The central truth which Paul brings to bear on the quarrels at Corinth is this: *The Church is Christ's Church*. The Church is one because Christ is One. There is only one Savior, only one Name.

The point is that if the Corinthians will think more deeply about their faith they will see how absurd it is to think of any man as *the* foundation. Apollos and Peter and Paul are like workmen on a farm; but it is God's farm, not theirs. They have different kinds of work. Paul the evangelist sows the seed; Apollos the teacher waters the crop. But it is as stupid to ask, Which is more important, Paul or Apollos? as it is to ask, Which is more important, to get the seed into the ground or to tend and water the growing plants?

The Key to Unity: the Message of the Cross (1:18—3:4)

But we are getting ahead of our story. Here, as usual, Paul does not lay down a series of neat propositions. He talks around and around, coming back to his main point from various angles, and also going off on ideas which at first sight seem to have little to do with this problem of unity. On the contrary, when more closely examined, these ideas are not side issues. He is still in the orbit of his main thought. Further, even if these matters can be considered parentheses or postscripts, the fact is that Paul often puts his most important and striking remarks into these "asides."

He gets into the "Message of the Cross" this way: first he asks (with some sarcasm) if Paul was crucified for them; or if they had been baptized into the name of Paul. Then he remarks that actually he baptized few people in Corinth. (This does not mean he thought little of baptism, only that he was not interested in doing this himself in every case.) This leads him to say what he *did* do, namely, preach the gospel. That was what God had commissioned him to do; that was his business.

God's Power and Wisdom Contrasted with Man's (1:18-31)

The message ("word") of the Cross is the power of God (1: 18); Christ crucified is "the power of God and the wisdom of God" (1:24), he is "our wisdom, our righteousness and sanctification and redemption" (1:30). That is the heart of this section (1:18-31).

We are so used to hearing this that we forget how shocking it sounded in Corinth in the mid-first century. The death of Jesus was an event which had occurred less than thirty years before this letter was written. Historically it was an execution of a "native" in a Roman province, by official order. The nature of the execution was such that every Roman thought of it as something done only to slaves and barbarians. (Roman citizens and aristocrats sometimes got condemned to death, but they were beheaded, not crucified.) Every Jew believed that anyone killed in that manner was under the curse of God.

Yet here was Paul, preaching not only that this Jesus was God's Son, and the Lord of all men, but that it was precisely *Christ crucified* who is God's Word to us, that this execution was actually the effect and the revelation of the grace and love of the true God. This was a "stumbling-block to Jews"—and no wonder. They could welcome a conquering Messiah but not a defeated one. They were eager for a king on a throne; but a man under a curse, a man on a cross, no. As for the Greeks, they could understand philosophy and high ideas, but their notion of God had no place for suffering in him. An executed peasant could not possibly stand for God or mean anything to cultivated men. Even if the sentence was an unjust one, to call such a man "Lord" was simply "folly to Gentiles."

Being himself a Jew, and educated in a Greek university, Paul knew just how Jews and Greeks (or Gentiles in general) would think about this. He knew how *he* used to think. So he draws these many contrasts between "the wisdom of the world" and "the folly of what we preach" (1:20-21); only the folly is not folly, it is the supreme wisdom of God. It is a "secret and hidden wisdom" (2:7) and not an obvious one. In the life—and death—

story of a poor carpenter in an obscure corner of the world, God has written his divine wisdom.

In using these words "wisdom" and "power" over and over, Paul is far from thinking of the Christian life merely as a special kind of knowledge, or of the Christian as a kind of philosopher with special enlightenment. God has made Christ our "righteousness and sanctification and redemption" (1:30). These words refer to life in full dimensions, not to the mind alone. Paul elsewhere says, "For to me to live is Christ" (Phil. 1:21), and tells the Colossians that Christ "is our life" (Col. 3:4). Here he says God is "the source of your life in Christ Jesus" (1:30). This sums up everything. But to one who reads the words for the first time they have a baffling sound. What can it mean to say Christ is our life, or that our life is "in" Christ?

At this point we may need some explanation if our twentieth-century minds are going to get anything out of Paul's first-century thought. There is a kind of religion—going under many names, but underneath always the same—known as "mysticism." The essence of mysticism is that the worshiper becomes one with the God he worships (or so he claims). There is no longer an "I" and a "Thou"; there is a complete blending or welding or transfusion. In the Hindu varieties of mysticism the slogan is, "Thou *art* That"; in at least one American variety of it, the preacher will tell the people, "You are cells of God." The idea of salvation, or the goal of the worshiper, is to lose his personal consciousness and realize his oneness with the All that we call God—like a spray of foam sinking back into the sea. Now Paul has been accused of "Christ-mysticism"; that is to say, it is thought by some people that Paul would say everything the mystic says, only in place of "God" Paul puts "Christ." Paul does use language that lays him open to this suspicion. "Christ is our life" is precisely what a Christ-mystic (and there have been such) would say.

Nevertheless, Paul was not a Christ-mystic in that extreme sense. The reader is invited, as he reads through the Corinthian correspondence and other writings of Paul, to observe the great amount of evidence for three propositions:

1. Paul does speak of the unity between Christ and the Christian, and among Christians, in very strong language (we find the same thought in John 15:1 and John 17). *But—*

2. For Paul, the individual never loses his individuality. I am

always I, not somebody else, not Christ, not God. Paul never suggests that he ceases to be Paul, or wants to cease being Paul. His great emphasis on the will, on choice and decision, on responsibility to God, all support the statement that for Paul salvation, the goal of human existence at its highest, is not to lose identity but to be "transformed"—into the *image* of Christ, yes, but not literally *into Christ*.

3. Paul never identifies Christ, numerically, with any Christian, or with the Church. Christ is intimately joined with the Christian, and is the Head of the Church; but Christ is never *the same as* the Christian or all Christians together.

So it is not quite fair to say that Paul is a "Christ-mystic." Nevertheless he does mean to say, and he says it in many ways, that Christ is the life of the Christian, or that the Christian's life is "in Christ." That last phrase has often been called the center and main point of Paul's conception of Christianity.

But a question must have occurred to the reader: What in the world has all this to do with the problem of quarrels in the church and how to get over them? In what way is the "word of the cross" (which for Paul is always the center of the truth about Christ) a key to Christian unity? It is quite simple: the Corinthian church was beginning to split up because its members were thinking in terms of men, leaders, parties, slogans, personalities. If they will put Christ as center of their thoughts and aspirations, if they will realize how it is *his* life—not Paul's nor Peter's nor any other man's—that flows into theirs and makes them over, then these quarrels will simply dry up and vanish.

How Paul Preached the Gospel (2:1-5)

We can now afford to run more rapidly through some other parts of this letter. In 2:1-5 Paul writes as if he never preached anything at all except the crucifixion of Christ. As a matter of fact, if his letters are any sample, what he means is that the Cross is a central point. In its light, problems are solved; by its light life's true direction is found. One point to note is that Paul does not present Christianity as a set of dogmas or as a manual of advice. It is a *story,* something that happened, something God has done.

Three Kinds of Men (2:6—3:4)

Some people in Corinth saw no point in Paul's preaching and

teaching. They did not get his meaning. Others did; and of these, some were greatly changed by it and others were changed but little. Paul has words (Greek, of course) for each of these kinds of men. There are no three words in English to match exactly these three Greek words. At the lowest level is the "unspiritual" man (2:14), or "natural" man (see margin), who is deaf to the gospel story and blind to Christ—and quite content to be so. The other two levels are those whose hearts have been touched by the Holy Spirit. But the middle level is of those who are undeveloped Christians, "babes in Christ" (3:1), Paul calls them. They are "in Christ"; they are on his side. But they have never lived up to their faith, nor appreciated it. At the top level are mature Christians. It was said of a certain Christian that he lived in a different "climate of the spirit" from other men. His whole attitude to life was "out of this world." He was a very practical man too, but he marched to the drums of heaven. The first-level men are like dead seed. The second-level men are like living plants, but stunted ones. The third level are the fruit-bearers. Show a light to a stone, and the stone does not change. Show a light to a baby and he will blink his eyes, but it does him little good. Show a light to a grown person and he will find his way by it.

God's Workmen, the Apostles; God's Workmanship, the Church (3:5—4:21)

The Apostles' Unity in Service (3:5-9)

You might expect, after all Paul's talk of "spiritual" and "unspiritual" men, that the "spiritual" were clear out of this world, that "spiritual" truths are so lofty they cannot be expressed in human language. Far from it. You can make a simple diagram to show Paul's idea here.

Unspiritual men: *discord, quarreling.*

Spiritual men: *harmony, unity.*

The "babes in Christ" are spiritual men who keep acting like unspiritual ones. Church quarrels are just as mean and unreasonable as any other kind of quarrel. It is unreasonable, and ridiculous too, to quarrel about which apostle is the Top Apostle. All three men whose names marked the parties in the Corinth church are simply God's workmen on God's farm, and the Corinthian Christians are the farm itself. The famous sentence, "We are fellow workmen for God," or better, "We are fellow workers *with* God" (3:9; see also margin), does not here mean Paul and the Corinthians, it means Paul and Apollos and Cephas.

The Church's Unity in Christ (3:10-23)

Without warning, Paul changes metaphors. He often does this in the middle of a stream of thought. A moment ago the Church was a field where God's laborers worked; now it is a building on which God's stonemasons are employed. (This is the passage back of the famous hymn, "The Church's One Foundation.") The building is a temple. Elsewhere Paul thinks of individual Christians' bodies as temples of the Holy Spirit (I Cor. 6:19), but here and in II Corinthians 6:16 it is the Christian community which is such a temple. At this point Paul puts in another word for Christian unity. To split a church is like wrecking a beautiful building. Indeed, splitting a church is one of the worst sins, just because the temple of God is holy.

Finally—yet not quite finally—Paul rises in an eloquent appeal: why do you quarrel as if Paul and Apollos and Peter were things to be owned and fought over? "All things are yours" (3:21)—all these leaders belong to all of you, they are not only God's servants but yours. That is all Paul needed to write, but he goes on in one of his great sayings: not only do these men belong to you, but so do the world, life, death, the present, the future. And they belong to you because you belong to Christ and Christ belongs to God.

The Humility of God's Servants (4:1-13)

We said "not quite finally" because Paul finds this the right place to say something more about servants of God, and apostles in particular, since an argument over their respective merits was precisely what started the trouble in Corinth. It should be clear that he means to include both Apollos and Peter as "apostles." This word "apostle" in the New Testament and the Early Church did not always have the specialized meaning it has come to bear in the Church. Paul here uses the word in a broader sense than the "Twelve Apostles." He means any leader in the Church sent by God. Elsewhere (as in Galatians and Second Corinthians)

Paul insists on his right to the title "apostle," but here he highlights other words. He has already said "workmen"; now he says
"servants" and "stewards" or "trustees." This was a good time
to remind the Corinthians that the apostles were by no means
so conceited about themselves as their partisans were. So Paul
reminds them that God is his judge, as he is of every man; that
before God we all stand on level ground.

Verses 8-13 are partly sarcasm. What Paul seems to be driving at is that so far from being Very Important Personages, the
apostles are at the bottom of the heap. The great difference between the apostles and the run-of-the-mine Corinthian Christians is
that the Corinthians were dead-end receivers of grace; like
babies, they thought only in terms of "What do I get out of it?"
Paul and other apostles were outgivers, sharers, builders, workers.

The Authority of a Father in Christ (4:14-21)

Yet Paul does not end on any humble-come-tumble note. He
reminds the Corinthians—and they needed to be told—that an
apostle is a man with authority. Yet this authority is not described as if Paul were arguing, from some church constitution,
just how much authority an apostle should have. He does not
describe himself in the manner of a bureaucrat in the Kingdom
of God or an officer in the army, his duties and responsibilities
carefully laid down. Still less does he look on himself as a judge.
He selects the word "father" to throw light on his authority. He
is the Corinthians' "father in Christ Jesus." In those days, more
than now, a father's word in a family was the last word; but in
those days just as much as now, a father could deal with his
boys "with a rod," or "with love in a spirit of gentleness" (4:21).
Paul may have to use the rod (and he did), but if he does, it will
be the fault of his children and not himself.

One more point in chapter 4 calls for a note. Is Paul a conceited egotist? His words sound like it: "Be imitators of me . . .
my ways in Christ, as I teach them everywhere." No one in the
twentieth-century Church—not even the Pope!—would talk like
that today. Did Paul think of himself as sinless, perfect, incapa-
ble of making a mistake? This is a sample of the places where our
knowledge of the situation and background shows us how to take
a remark like the one in 4:16. The people to whom he was writing were completely without any Christian background. The
Christian religion itself was young, younger than most Christians

were. Paul could not say, imitate your Christian parents—none of them had had Christian parents. He could not say, imitate Jesus, for not a single Gospel had yet been written. He could give them rules, but if Paul made anything clear, it was that Christianity is not a rulebook religion. (Romans was largely written around that point.) The most practical way Paul had of pointing those raw, immature Christians of Corinth to a Christian example, was to point to one Christian they knew and respected —himself. As for Paul's considering himself beyond criticism, he has just been telling them (4:3-4) that while he himself has a clear conscience, this does not prove anything, it does not acquit him; it is God who is his judge. Later on in this letter Paul refers to himself as a man "who by the Lord's mercy is trustworthy" (7:25). It is in this spirit that he can invite his friends to follow his example.

IMMORALITY OF CHURCH MEMBERS; LAWSUITS AMONG CHRISTIANS; CHURCH DISCIPLINE

I Corinthians 5:1—6:20

Every counselor and every psychiatrist knows that very often the person who comes with a problem actually is troubled by some deeper problem that he does not mention. It was so with the church at Corinth. They had written Paul a letter (as we have noted) asking his advice on sundry problems. But none of the problems they mentioned involved the questioners in downright sins. They must have shown up in that letter as puzzled people, eager to know what was right. But before Paul gets to the problems they mention, he deals with some they do not mention. And these do involve sin, any way you take them. One, we have seen, was the quarreling spirit so many of them showed. Another was a very serious case of adultery and incest combined, a man living with his stepmother.

The points Paul makes are two: first, this is a serious wickedness, so bad it would shock respectable pagans. Second, and just as bad, the church at Corinth has done nothing whatever about it. He condemns them severely on both counts.

It does not excuse the Corinthians but it may help to explain this bad state of affairs if we keep remembering when all this took place. Keep in mind the date, well before A.D. 60, and the place, a city that even in the easygoing Roman Empire was notorious for sex perversions and sex crimes. Keep in mind also what Paul has said about the membership of that church. "Not many of you were wise according to worldly standards, not many were powerful, not many were of noble birth" (1:26). The church members were not only Corinthians, they were low-class Corinthians. They had been Corinthians for many years before they became Christians. All missionaries have found that when a convert comes out of a pagan background he generally brings some of that background with him, especially its moral standards.

Explain it as we may, it is not to excuse what Paul found inexcusable. There were enough people in that church, he felt, to realize that this particular kind of thing was wrong, so wrong that the guilty person ought not to be kept in the church any longer. Further, the church had the authority to expel this offender. Drive out the wicked man! Paul does not use soft words about it.

Let us look at one difficulty in this chapter, and then consider some problems it raises for our own situations. Nearly everything in this section is straightforward, needing little if any explanation; all but the second paragraph (vss. 3-5) and possibly a bit of the third (vss. 6-8). The meaning of verses 3-5 may be this: "If I were with you I know just what I would do. I have thought about it so much I can picture myself at your meeting. So when you do meet, just leave a vacant chair and think of me in it. Then you are to put this man out of the church, solemnly and for his own good. You are to put him back in the kingdom of Satan where he came from. I do not think this will doom him for all eternity. Indeed, you will be doing this to save the man's soul." But how would putting a man out of the church, simply turning your back on him and leaving him to the Devil—how could that help a man who had sinned? Paul does not say, and gives no hints. We may guess that what he meant was that such rough treatment would bring the man to his senses; that being put out of the fellowship of Christians would make him appreciate the Church as never before; that the kingdom of Satan would shock him as it never used to when he was a real part of it; that he would truly repent and be glad if the day came when the Christians could take him into their midst again.

Have these bygones any practical meaning for us today? At this point we ought to stop and consider a problem which meets us over and over again as we read Paul's letters. Do these long-dead-and-gone problems mean anything to us in our twentieth-century churches? First Corinthians is one long letter about problems. The first one we discovered was the business of church quarrels. This is plainly for us—not that Paul literally had us in mind when he wrote about the factions in Corinth, but as we (so to speak) eavesdrop on some confidential remarks Paul is making to his quarrelsome friends, we are struck by the fact that his analysis of church quarrels, their cause and cure, is remarkably modern. So long as churchmen squabble, so long will Paul's words about squabbling Christians be strictly up-to-date.

But what about such problems as this one of the man who lived with his stepmother? It surely would be a rare church that had that particular problem on its hands today. As we proceed through Paul's letters, and especially First Corinthians, we shall discover other problems that no doubt kept that Apostle awake nights, but they would be most uncommon today. Shall we just skip those parts of the letter? What can we make of these out-of-date worries?

We can find every part of Paul's letters helpful if we use the principle of *analogy*. That is, the problem before us may not be exactly the same as any we have today. But if we have the same *kind* of problem, we can obtain valuable help from Paul on how to deal with it.

Again, we can often identify a *principle* on which Paul operates to solve his problem. Since Paul's principles were always lofty ones—indeed, the Church has always taken them as revealed to Paul by God himself—we should never hesitate to use those same principles in solving the difficulties of our own experience.

It is safe to say that the Church would never have preserved these letters of Paul to Corinth if they had not been convinced, down the Christian centuries, that Paul's words reached far beyond his day and time, and that in his reactions to the troubles of the church in Corinth (and churches elsewhere too) he was illuminating not only those specific problems but also those of the long road ahead, the road of which we do not yet see the end.

Then what about this case of incest? What Paul says about it throws light on two perennial problems. The first of these is the problem of *moral standards in the Christian Church.* Paul was plagued by people who twisted his words (as Peter said) to their own destruction. Readers of Romans will remember how carefully Paul laid it down that we cannot earn the favor of God, that we are saved by grace, not by our own merits or goodness. Faith is the acceptance of God's acceptance, of his taking us, each one, just as we are. No doubt Paul had preached this in Corinth as he wrote it to Rome. Many would misunderstand this. They would say, "Then it makes no difference what I do; God accepts me regardless. As God's loving child I can do what I please." You have to stop reading each of Paul's letters long before you reach the end of it to get notions like that. In every letter Paul writes he makes it clear, just as our Lord did, that a Christian is not only *not* exempt from the moral law, he is held to a higher standard than anyone else. As a child of God he should be growing into God-likeness. Paul was interested, furthermore, in the reputation of the Church outside, in the world. Some religions of that era were morally bad; they had no decent person's respect. It would be a tragedy if the new religion of Christ should be confused in men's minds with these wild "religions." Evangelism becomes a very bad thing if it invites people into a kind of club whose members are, so to speak, licensed practitioners of wickedness!

The second problem is that of *the authority of the Church.* But who is going to be responsible for keeping up the moral standards of the Church? This is the responsibility of the whole Church, Paul tells us. It will not do to leave the Church in the kind of mess it becomes when everybody does as he pleases. Standards must be maintained, and high ones; and the Church as a whole must maintain them. One way, a last resort perhaps, is to excommunicate; that is, to remove from its fellowship persons who deliberately and stubbornly refuse to live as Christ's men and women. Perhaps such persons have never really been converted; then they had no business in the Church to begin with. Perhaps they are Christians at heart; in that case being shut out of the fellowship of Christ's people for a time will bring them to themselves.

One interesting and important point here concerns the authority of the Church. This act of punishment and discipline, expelling a wicked man, is not to be done by one person (not even by Paul himself), nor by committee action. It is the affair of the whole

Church. The authority of the Church does not come from the top down; it comes from the ground up. The authority of the Church is not in a hierarchy; it is in the people. If a minister or a session or a board or council or classis or presbytery—whatever it may be called—acts in cases of discipline or otherwise, it is action representing the Church as a whole. The authority *of* the Church is *in* the Church, in all its parts. Paul does not complain that some committee failed to act in the case he is discussing. He does not excuse them for failure to act on the ground that no Apostle could be present and therefore no action could be taken. He lays the blame on the people to whom he was writing, the whole congregation of Christians in the local church where the outrage had occurred. The disgrace had come to the Church as a whole, and the Church as a whole had the right and duty to deal with the case.

Paul comes back to the question of morals (6:9-11) after dealing with the lawsuit problem. Taken in the context of all his teaching, we can be sure he does *not* mean: (1) that anyone who ever commits one of these sins is thereby shut out forever from the Kingdom; or (2) that a converted person never can commit any of these sins. What he does mean is that one who commits these sins (and, doubtless, others not spoken of here) by that act steps out of the Kingdom; and to keep on committing them is to stay out of the Kingdom.

Still on the theme of morals, Paul comments (6:12) on the expression, "All things are lawful for me [because I am saved]." We shall return to this later. He then singles out sexual sin as especially evil, because it is a sin (1) against one's own body, (2) against one's spirit (vss. 16-17), (3) against the Holy Spirit (vs. 19), and (4) against the God who actually suffered to win men back to himself. This is a perfect illustration of how Paul never solves problems by trivial ways or by appealing to trivial motives. "You are not your own." That is the high and sufficient answer to all the twaddle about "All things are lawful for me"— that is, to the idea that I can do as I please. As God's own, the Christian is free—to do what God pleases. Christian freedom is *in* God and *under* God; it is not freedom *from* God.

The section on lawsuits (6:1-8), which has been passed over, is plain enough without commentary. It provides a good illustration of the fact that very few Christians take all that Paul says literally, as if he were laying down exact rules for life today. He

assumes that all law courts are operated by heathen persons, that
judges, officers, lawyers, are all non-Christian and perhaps anti-
Christian. Most courts in America, and in many other countries,
are presided over by Christian judges, who may even be officers
in the Church. If you lived in a country where the Christian
Church was extremely small and where law courts were strongly
non-Christian, you would have a situation like the one in Corinth,
and would be right in following Paul's advice literally. But this
is not advice that is followed by American Christians; it does not
fit our situation. A great many questions at law are so complex
anyway that it would be absurd to expect a church meeting
to settle them.

However, the context of Paul's thought is not the complexities
of our industrial age. He is speaking to a group of people, small
and closely knit, all of whom know all the others. In a family
group like that, going to law anywhere, at any time, is out of line
with true Christian relationships. Disputes arising between Christians in the same church family ought never to arrive at the law
court stage. If we cannot settle peaceably our differences—and
Christians have always had them—we have no moral right to
lecture "the world" for its lack of love.

SEX AND MARRIAGE

I Corinthians 7:1-40

Paul now turns to the problems the Corinthians themselves had
raised when writing him. It is not surprising that the pressing
problem on their list was sex and marriage. The Jews had for
centuries held and practiced a high ideal of sex and family life.
Some of the plainest commandments in the Old Testament have
to do with sex. The Gentiles of early Christian times, on the
other hand, were among the most loose-living people of history,
especially when it came to liquor and sex. One of the leading Roman biographers of Julius Caesar admired that general, among
other things, for his "chastity." By that he meant only that Caesar
was not a homosexual; his relations with women were promiscu-
ous. Now when people like the Romans came into the same religious community with the Jews, there was bound to be a clash
of opinions on the right and wrong of sex and marriage. Paul, of
course, upheld the Jewish ideals. He believed, and we believe with

him, that God had already shown mankind, through the Jews who were bearers of his word to the world, what the divine intention for man is in this vital aspect of his life. That intention, in a word, is: before marriage, continence; in marriage, faithfulness throughout life. But of course this general principle did not settle all the questions.

Before looking at some details, we need a little background. (1) This whole chapter is neither Paul's last nor his best word about marriage. It undoubtedly represented his sincere view at the time, but by the time he wrote Ephesians he had come to a much higher conception of Christian marriage. The best he can say for marriage in this entire chapter 7 is that it is no sin. He concedes that marriage is necessary for most persons, but only to avoid fornication. Marriage for Paul seems a concession to the necessities of weak-willed people. (2) He draws on his own experience, as he often does, to form his conclusions. He argues that unmarried people are happier than married people, for he has found it so himself. It is a question often asked: Was Paul ever married? Obviously not at the time he wrote this letter. Many scholars believe that Paul had been a member of the Sanhedrin (the high court) at Jerusalem, and that therefore he must have been married, as bachelors were not admitted to this high position. Perhaps he had had a wife who left him, or died. To the mind of your commentator (who of course knows no more about this than others do!), all that Paul says about marriage in this chapter suggests that he had been through a marriage that almost but never quite succeeded—a marriage which he felt interfered with his spiritual life, a marriage in which it had been impossible to be both a good husband and a good Christian missionary (7:32-35). By the time he wrote Ephesians, he could actually think of marriage as an illustration of the relation between Christ and the Church, something quite far from his thought in the Corinthian letter. Had he seen a real Christian marriage in the home of Aquila and Priscilla? Had he perhaps met some Christian woman who opened a window in his heart? We can only speculate, remembering that Ephesians 5, not I Corinthians 7, is Paul's last word on marriage. (3) Paul was still at this time expecting the end of all things to come to pass in his own lifetime—and soon. The advice he gives on marriage is not given with an eye to long years ahead for individuals or nations or the human race, but rather for the short time before the final catastrophe. If you had pointed out to him that if his wish came true and everyone felt just as he did, happiest when unmarried, and with no wish or need to marry, then the human race would soon disappear, Paul would not have been embarrassed. "Coming generations" is a phrase the Old Testament uses (or words to that effect), but not Paul till he was older than when writing this letter, not till the long years had given him another perspective.

The advice Paul gives to the unmarried and the married can be summed up in a few sentences, all but one difficult paragraph. We can make it clear by outlining it.

1. To the unmarried (including widows): Stay as you are; that is better (7:8-9). It is better for a man not to live with a woman at all. But if you find this to be impossible, then get married; it is no sin, and enormously better than fornication or constantly burning desire. Whether you are a bachelor or a spinster, a widow or a widower, whether you never had a wife or lost the one you had through death, desertion, or divorce, no matter; *stay as you are*. As a single person, you will be happier and better able to serve the Lord with an undivided mind.

2. To the married: Stay as you are. Do not leave your wife or husband; do not drive away your partner; do not refuse to live with her, or him, as if you were not married at all. Suppose you are married to an unbeliever? Still stay as you are. If your partner stays, you can be a blessing to him (her) and to the children (7:14-16). If your partner leaves, and in Corinth this would be very common, let him (her) go in peace. Be reconciled if you can (7:11); otherwise realize that you are always in a better state when single.

3. To men who have virgins for whom they are responsible. This is the puzzling section of this chapter (vss. 36-38). Under what circumstances would a man be in charge of a virgin without being married to her? Commentators are not agreed about this. Most translations are interpretations at this point; "betrothed" is one interpretation: the Greek word is simply "virgin." A strict translation of the Greek casts no light on the question. There are two main interpretations: (a) the man and the virgin are father and daughter; (b) the man and the virgin are an engaged couple. The latter is the interpretation of the Revised Standard Version. (A variety of the second interpretation, held by some Bible students, is that the man and girl are living in a kind of

celibate marriage, that is, marriage in name only, without inter-course. We do know that such marriages were sometimes tried out by Christians at a later period. The idea was to "spiritualize" marriage entirely. The Church finally forbade such experiments.) In the Greek of this passage there are difficulties with each of these theories. In this writer's opinion, there are fewer difficulties with (b) than with (a). In any case, Paul's advice is just what would be expected from what he has already said. Let the virgin remain a virgin ("Stay as you are"), unless there is desire beyond control, in which case marriage is to be advised. Paul here repeats his point, "He who refrains from marriage will do better" (I Cor. 7:38).

FOOD FROM IDOLS' TEMPLES: CAN HARMLESS ACTS BE WRONG?
I Corinthians 8:1—11:1

We now come to a section of this letter which, perhaps more than most, shows the characteristic Pauline touches. First of all, he starts with a real and practical problem and finally reaches some practical answers. But he finds his answer by way of a high principle which, as he shows us, is bound up with the nature of Christianity itself. Furthermore, as he develops the theme, his train of thought goes off into various sidetracks. He discusses ministers' salaries, he analyzes his own motives in the ministry, he discusses conscience and the communion table. Here is no formal essayist, but a man with an active mind writing, or more likely dictating, as he talks, and talking as he thinks. Since Paul did not write from an outline, like a professor, we must admit that here as elsewhere our outlines may not exactly fit the exciting movement of Paul's mind.

The Problem

Readers of Romans will recognize the problem and know already in advance what Paul's conclusions will be, in general. It was the universal problem that Christians faced in those days, of the meat for sale in the butcher shops everywhere. It was ex-tremely likely that the animal from which the steak or chop had been taken had been killed as a temple sacrifice in some heathen

religion. The nub of the problem was this: If I eat such meat, am
I participating in the worship of idols? Can a Christian eat such
meat and remain a Christian?

The First Answer (8:1-6)

Paul's first answer is soon out. Briefly: an idol has no real existence. It is like a doll. Nothing happens to meat if it has been
used "playing house" with dolls; so with idols. "We are no worse
off if we do not eat, and no better off if we do" (8:8). It is not
possible to offer meat or anything else to another "god," for
there are no other gods.

Here Paul breaks into what is grammatically an aside, yet is
one of the key thoughts of the entire Bible: ". . . for us there is
one God, the Father, from whom are all things and for whom we
exist, and one Lord, Jesus Christ, through whom are all things
and through whom we exist" (vs. 6).

A Second Answer (8:7-13)

The trouble is, not everybody can see the point Paul has made
about there being only one God. Corinthian Gentiles would have
lived too long with the belief that gods are many, to get over
that belief quickly. In the minds of these persons there would be
a feeling of guilt. This might be irrational, but the feeling would
be there all the same. Children used to have a game of jumping
over the cracks in a sidewalk. Something bad was supposed to
happen if you stepped on a crack; and if anything bad did happen, as occurs nearly every day, the other children would say,
"Aha, we told you . . . now you're to blame for this mess." Some
little children have been made to feel very miserable, guilty of
something that was not bad at all. But their consciences hurt
them just as much as if their "sin" had been real.

Now, Paul says, you know and I know that eating this meat is
neither here nor there. God will never ask you where the meat
came from. It is no more a matter of conscience than saying
"rare" or "well done." The trouble is, some people are upset by
your eating, they think you a sinner and lose respect for you; or,
on the other hand, they may venture to eat because you did, and
then their conscience hurts. No use saying their conscience ought
not to hurt, because it does and they can't help it. Say all you

please about their heathen background, they can't help that either. You are leading some people into going against their consciences, and to go against conscience is always wrong.

Well, someone would say, in this case the conscience itself is wrong. Do you mean to say I must give up my freedom just because somebody's conscience makes a mountain out of a molehill? Is the conscience of these weak-minded, ignorant people any concern of mine?

Indeed it is; Paul emphasizes the point. These weak-minded persons are brothers "for whom Christ died" (8:11). You are enlightened, intelligent; you know the truth, that meat is meat and there is no idolatry in it. You know it is no sin to eat it. But if your freedom is causing someone else to go against his conscience, you are actually destroying that man's character. Remember, that man is your brother. So that is the second answer: "Therefore, if food is a cause of my brother's falling, I will never eat meat, lest I cause my brother to fall" (8:13; see also Rom. 14).

Paul thus shifts the whole question to a different level. If you ask the question in the form, What can I do without harm to myself? you can get one answer; in this case, Go and eat. But if you ask it in the form, What does my action do to other persons? then the answer is: Do nothing that breaks down their character. Do not let your freedom be a sin against your brothers. A Christian should never stop at the first level; he should go on to the second. "What am I doing to me?" is a fair question; but above and beyond it is the question, "What am I doing to others?"

Paul's Good Example (9:1-27)

Paul now points to his own example, not about this particular problem—he seems to feel enough has been said about it already —but about a larger problem, showing how this principle works out in a more important matter than beefsteaks. As we would put it today, this is the question of the minister's salary. Those were early days when precedents were being made. The economic side of the New Testament story is one we overlook because it is so seldom mentioned. But all these saints, apostles, and martyrs had to live. Somehow they had to have money for groceries. Where did it come from? Few if any of the apostles were well-to-do. From all the hints we have in the New Testament, it would appear that the traveling apostles lived by freewill offerings from the people in the various churches. Paul defends this practice in 9:1-12a. He has not changed the subject; he is still on the basic issue: Can a "right"—that is to say, a permissible, approved, correct, harmless act—still be wrong? Is a Christian sometimes obliged, for the sake of others, to refrain from doing what would be, for him, a good act? Paul has shown that the Christian is always bound to think of the effect of his act on others, and has applied this principle to the problem of the dubious beefsteaks. Now he takes an example from his own practice as a traveling preacher. He has a perfect right, he says, to do what the other missionaries do. Cephas (Peter) and others accept money not only for their own expenses but for their wives as well (9:3-6). He draws a parallel from other fields of work: the worker can expect to be paid from the business itself (9:7-12). He points out especially that the priests of the Temple get their living from the Temple offerings (9:13). Finally he brings up a directive from the Lord Jesus himself, who when sending out the Twelve told them to expect that the places where they would stay would supply food and lodging (9:14; see Luke 10:7-8).

And yet, though to accept his support from the Church would be right, and in fact just what Christ commanded, Paul will not use his right. He wants to "make the gospel free of charge" (9:18). Paul no doubt knew, what many ministers since his time have discovered, that there are people both outside and inside the Church who have a suspicion that the minister has to say what he says because he is paid to say it. Paul would rather be in a position where everyone would know that he never received a penny from any man. "Whose bread I eat, his song I sing," runs an old proverb that Corinth would have understood. Paul wanted to make it very clear, by supporting himself with his own hands (by tentmaking, as is well known), that the bread he ate was his own, and his song was his own. To be sure, he did feel a strong obligation to preach (9:16), but it was a different kind of necessity from a bread-and-butter one. His main driving interest was to "persuade men," as he put it elsewhere. "I do it all for the sake of the gospel" (9:23).

Some modern writer has said that the minute a man insists on comfort he has given up his independence. Paul renounced comfort for the sake of independence. He does not claim it was easy. The language he uses in 9:25-27 shows that it has been a fight.

All the pictures of early Christians make them look thin. Well, they *were* thin. Paul's body no doubt cried out for food and rest that were not possible. But Paul said, "I pommel my body and subdue it"; he would treat it as his slave rather than be himself his body's slave.

Paul says in 9:27 that he pommels (beats on) and subdues his body lest he himself "should be disqualified." Does he mean he does not feel assured of his own salvation? The Greek word which is translated "disqualified" means literally "rejected," "disapproved." It does not mean eternally lost. Paul wanted to be more than barely saved; he wanted the "Well done!" of the Master. The whole sweep and swing of Paul's letter shows that he really had no doubt of his own salvation. Christ had died for him, he was sure. What he does at times feel anxious about is whether God approves him, whether he is one of God's honored servants or only a tolerated one. Paul wants not only personal approval, he wants also God's high rating for his work. A person may be a true Christian by intention and yet do mighty sloppy work for the Lord. Paul did not want to be one of those people.

A Bad Example from Ancient Israel (10:1-13)

Chapter 10 starts off in such a way as to puzzle the reader. Is Paul changing the subject again? And if not, what have the ancient Israelites got to do with meat offered to idols, and with the motives of a preacher? It is clear that Paul does not think he has left the problem of chapter 8 behind, because he speaks directly to it before the chapter ends. One way to connect this chapter 10 with 8 and 9 is suggested in our outline. After giving his own example of refusing to accept gifts which he had every right to accept—and doing it all for the sake of the gospel—Paul now gives the example of people who were strictly selfish, the very well-known example of the Israelites in the desert. They were so selfish, greedy, and comfort-loving that not even a prophet of God could make heroes out of them, and all God could do was to let them die in the desert. In short, it may be that Paul intends this as a warning to those who thought only of themselves and asked only the question, Will this hurt *me?*

There are other possible interpretations. An attractive one is this: Paul may be wanting to say a word to the kind of Christian whom he has already addressed as a superior type, freed from the superstitious fears that afflict the consciences of the ignorant. These are Christians who appreciate their freedom in Christ. Paul may be warning them not to presume on their favored position. He may be bringing up the example of the Israelites who, though God's people, failed to please God. These "superior" Christians found it odd, no doubt, that anyone would be afraid to eat meat that had been offered to idols. Be careful, Paul may be saying to them. You can fall into idolatry yourself. If the Israelites of old, who surely had witnessed the power of the true God, could fall into worshiping a golden calf, you need not think *you* are too high a type to do anything so silly or sinful.

At all events, Paul comes back from ancient to contemporary days and problems. "Let any one who thinks that he stands take heed lest he fall" (10:12), is plain enough for everybody. And then he adds a comforting thought to balance his warning: "God . . . will not let you be tempted beyond your strength" (10:13).

Here is another beautiful example of Paul's way of starting from some problem you and I will never meet in our lives, something now totally obsolete, and coming out at something universal. Human conceit, human temptation and weakness, God's protecting providence—here are thoughts for Everyman.

Summing Up (10:14—11:1)

With 10:14 Paul takes a new line, though still on the same problem. Some who read chapter 8 might think that Paul took idolatry lightly, so he makes it quite clear that he sees this as a serious sin. Sacrificing to idols is in fact sacrificing to demons. Some Bible students think Paul meant that each separate idol was actually one personal demon or devil, who seduced human beings to worship him. A more likely meaning is twofold: (1) Few if any of the "gods" worshiped in a pagan city at that era would be thought of, even by the worshipers, as the High God, the God of gods; indeed, the Greek word for demon was sometimes used for these imaginary creatures. (2) Whatever demons there be are surely delighted when men worship anything but the true God. To worship at any idol's shrine is to contribute to the Devil's delight. So the idols represent demons in general, rather than each idol being really one particular demon.

At any rate, it is clear that Paul teaches, on the one hand, that idolatry is a serious sin, totally inconsistent with being a Christian at all; but on the other hand, that meat in the market is simply meat, just the same wherever it came from. The sensible thing to do is to buy it and not ask where it was killed. If you *know* it came from a heathen temple, and you know that other Christians know it and are disturbed by it, then remember what has already been said: You are not your own, you have others to consider. Paul sums it all up in one noble sentence: "I try to please all men in everything I do, not seeking my own advantage, but that of many, that they may be saved" (10:33).

First Corinthians 10:16-22 is a little confusing, but the general meaning should be clear: Christianity and pagan religion are represented here by the Communion on the one side, the pagan sacrifices on the other. Paul does not mean that the Communion is a sacrifice. He is drawing a contrast, not a parallel, between pagan and Christian faith and worship. You simply cannot be both pagan and Christian.

"Be imitators of me" (11:1) sounds egotistic, and it is true that Paul was no shrinking violet. But what else could Paul recommend? He could not say, "Read your Gospels and imitate Christ," because the Gospels had not been written. He, Paul, was the best sample of Christianity the Corinthians knew, and it was a practical way of saying to those very simple Corinthians, Be Christian.

PUBLIC WORSHIP: BAD AND GOOD WAYS

I Corinthians 11:2-34

The next section of this letter, which was written by Paul to settle matters, has turned out to be one of the hotbeds of argument in the Church. This short commentary cannot even begin to say what the arguments are. Whatever can be said about almost any verse in chapter 11 is and has been vigorously disputed somewhere in the Christian Church. With due respect for different views, what follows comes from a point of view not peculiar to your commentator but one which is a growing view in the Church.

Women's Place in the Church (11:2-16)

This chapter (see also 14:34-36) gives a striking example of the difference between temporary and permanent elements in the teaching of Paul. Two opposite views can be discarded: one, that everything Paul wrote is everlastingly binding on the Christian Church; two, that all of Paul's writing is of historic interest but no longer authoritative any more than are utterances of any early Christian missionary or bishop. The middle view is that some things Paul said concerned local conditions and do not hold in our changed situation. Other things he said are universal, irreplaceable, and for all Christians the last word. Even in the temporary and local directives of Paul there are basic principles which are as sound now as they ever were.

What Paul says about women, a great deal of it, comes under the head of advice which is not for us today. We shall go through the paragraph (11:2-16) briefly, simply pointing out what Paul actually says, letting the reader make his own comments if he (or she) will. (1) Woman is definitely subordinate to man. The order is, from bottom to top: woman, man, Christ, God. (2) It is only man, not woman, who is the "glory" of God. (3) Woman was created for the benefit of man, not the other way around. (As we would express it, this is a man's world and God meant it to be so.) (4) Any woman who prays or "prophesies," that is, "preaches," without a veil is acting in a disgraceful manner. Please note that Paul is speaking of veils, not hats. (5) Nature teaches that long hair is a disgrace to a man but a matter of pride for a woman. This suggests that women should be veiled.

In 14:34-36, Paul forbids women to speak in church, absolutely. It has always been a puzzle to commentators to know whether chapter 11 or chapter 14 is what Paul meant: Should women speak only when veiled, or not at all?

At any rate, the Protestant Church today, in practice, has departed from these regulations of Paul, and indeed from this view of women in general. Paul has the point of view of first-century Judaism, which he did not leave behind when he became a Christian. Nevertheless, for Corinth in the first century, this was first-class practical advice; we should not go wrong in calling it inspired. Corinth was a place where a woman had to be very careful to maintain a good reputation. The place was crawling with slimy "religions" which were no better than nests of vice. Christianity had a reputation to make. If it was known that in meetings of Christians women sat around without veils, and that they even *talked*—two things no respectable first-century lady would do outside her own family circle—the Christian religion would have been labeled at once as an outfit no dignified and decent person would want to join.

So, not everything that can be wisely done today could wisely be done in Corinth. Yet we can think of this now outmoded advice as part of the "Word of God." Your mother told you, when you were small, "Don't touch matches." When you went to college, or when you got married, your mother did not repeat that order about the matches. Yet it was your mother's word to you. So God's word to Corinth, through the mind and pen of Paul, may not be his word to Chicago or Toronto today. It is not that God has changed his mind, but that the Church has grown up.

Disunity (11:17-22)

We may be almost thankful for the quarrels and conceit and disorderliness with which the Corinthian church observed Communion, for it was in dealing with their disgraceful behavior that one of the most vital and best-loved passages of the New Testament was written.

First we have what is to us a shocking and almost incredible picture (11:17-22) of a church meeting which, Paul says, actually made the "worshipers" worse and not better. The congregation was, as we already know, split up into factions. Perhaps those he mentions in chapter 1 are the same as those of this paragraph in chapter 11, perhaps not. But anyhow the picture here reminds us more of a badly organized Sunday school picnic than of a Communion service.

Indeed, it was not entirely a Communion service. Besides that, for a long time in the early Christian Church there was observed a ceremony known as the "love feast." When they finally got it regulated, it was more solemn and formal than a picnic by far, yet it was not the same as the Communion.

But at the time Paul was writing, there had been no regulations. All the Corinthians knew about the feast was that it was a good thing to express the idea of the Church as a *family* by having a meal together. Only they did not have it together. They gathered in little knots, rich people by themselves with fancy dishes, poor people and even slaves by themselves, without enough for a good sandwich. Some rich people would even make a cocktail party out of it and go home drunk (Paul spares no words), while others afterwards would go to bed hungry.

Probably these Corinthians mixed up the love feast with the Communion, for Paul goes on at once to speak of that.

The Lord's Supper (11:23-34)

The next paragraph (11:23-26) is among the most cherished and familiar passages of the entire Bible. There are four stories of the Last Supper in the Upper Room in the New Testament, the other three being in Matthew, Mark, and Luke. But Paul wrote before any of the others. This is the very first story ever written of the first Lord's Supper. It is familiar to all of us, for it is Paul's story rather than any other which is usually read at the Communion service. Since the reader has probably heard many sermons based on it, no long comment is needed here. It is for meditation rather than analysis. A few points may be underscored. (1) This observance is not yet called a sacrament. The thing itself is older than all names for it except simply "the Lord's Supper." (2) It is not called a "sacrifice." It is a remembrance and a proclamation. (3) Nothing is said about a presiding officer. Emphasis is on the participants as a group. (4) There is no support here, except by the most bald literal interpretation, for the notion that the bread and wine were, or ever are, actually changed into the body and blood of our Lord. (5) Nevertheless, the symbols are those of violent death—a broken body, blood poured out upon the ground. (6) Yet this is not a mere recollection of a tragedy; it is an expression of a glorious hope. In this observance, memory and hope mingle in a common glory—memory of the Lord's life freely given for us; hope of the Lord's return, of his final reign.

Paul warns against eating the bread and drinking the cup of the Lord "in an unworthy manner" (11:27). Strictly speaking, no human being is "worthy" of what Christ has done for him; none is worthy to take part in the Communion. What Paul means is shown by his previous condemnation of the way the Corinthian church "observed" or rather defamed this sacrament. We take Communion in an unworthy manner—that is, in a manner that degrades it and does not lift us any nearer God— when we enter into it thoughtlessly, or with thoughts and attitudes which we know are not Christlike and yet we cling to them. Pride, selfishness, scorn of those we ought to help—in short, the loveless heart—all this is part of the sin from which Communion should turn us. That we have these sins may be true. If we *cling* to them, Communion is not for us. If we turn from them with genuine grief, this *is* for us.

Here is also a warning against not "discerning the body" (11:29). The traditional interpretation of this is that "body" refers to the broken body of Christ. In other words, if anyone takes part in the Communion seeing in it only something we have to do because Jesus said do it, or making it into just another ceremony of the Church, or a rededication, without realizing that it is Christ's death we here celebrate, he misses the point, he really does not celebrate Communion. On the other hand, there is another explanation of this warning. Not discerning the body, to some Bible scholars, means not perceiving the Body of Christ, that is, the Church. On this interpretation, an individualistic attitude to the Lord's Supper violates an essential principle of it, namely, that it is something shared. Taking Communion is not a matter between the soul and God alone; it is between Christian brother and Christian brother. If you try to see God without looking at your brother, you are not celebrating *Communion* even if you call it by that name.

Incidentally, verse 30 can be taken literally, but it seems better to take it spiritually. Some of the Corinthians are weak in soul and ill in spirit; they have taken "Communion" in a spirit of selfish meanness, and so they have not only profaned what God has given them, they have also denied the very spirit and meaning of it all. No wonder their souls are shriveled.

SPIRITUAL GIFTS; WORSHIP (CONTINUED)

I Corinthians 12:1—14:39

It is hard for us in the twentieth century to realize how absolutely *new* the Christian religion was when Paul wrote these letters. Take one single ordinary question: What do these Christians do when they get together for meetings? Nowadays that sounds like a silly question. Everyone knows about "church services." They are so regular, so much in one groove, that there is an "order of service" made long in advance; the minister's sermon will perhaps be typed days ahead of time; and if you have been there before, you can take next Sunday's service bulletin and figure almost to the minute what the congregation will be doing at any particular time between 11 and 12 o'clock.

Not so in the first century; not at all so in Corinth. If you had dropped in on them some Lord's Day, you would have perhaps been embarrassed, certainly confused. A feeling of tension, of great excitement, would pervade the meeting. Everybody would seem to be talking at once. You might understand ordinary Greek, but you would discover that some of these people were shouting strange sounds that nobody could understand. If you hung around and talked after the meeting, you would discover that these people attributed their excitement, and their talking and shouting, even the unintelligible noises, to the Holy Spirit. You would find that the people who talked in this odd fashion, if it could be called "talk," were rather proud of it, and in fact considered that this "speaking in tongues" as they called it was a special mark of distinction. You might overhear an argument between one of the "tongues" speakers and another man who claimed to have healed six people that week just by laying his hands on them. Another member might be claiming that the Holy Spirit's "gift" to a speaker you could understand was greater than his gift to one you could not.

One thing is sure. If you went through a modern congregation asking, "Have you any spiritual gifts?" you might get some glassy stares. But at Corinth you would get eager replies, "Yes, yes, I've got the greatest!" We do not know how much they had written Paul about this, but he writes to this confused, excited situation. There is no doubt that they *wanted* the "gifts" —the powers, strange and impressive—of the Spirit. The question was, How can we know they *are* gifts of the Holy Spirit? There were other religions with somewhat similar features. And there is a further question: What are the principal gifts? What powers should we want most to have?

Spiritual Gifts (12:1-11)

In writing on this problem Paul lays down some plain, practical principles, fresh and forceful as the day they were first put on paper. Furthermore, in discussing the question Paul rises to a height of eloquence and insight he seldom if ever equals; the great and famous chapter on love comes right in the middle of what he has to say about spiritual gifts and the worship of God. Most of this needs no commentary, as it is simple and plain.

First, Paul says what is more obvious to us than it was, perhaps, at Corinth: No one can curse Jesus and claim to be speaking by the Spirit. On the other hand, no one can say, "Jesus is Lord," except by the Holy Spirit. Of course any wicked person could repeat those words, but what Paul means is that no one can sincerely accept Jesus as Lord of his life, his Number One authority, except by the Holy Spirit. This broadens the idea of "spiritual" beyond the limits which many of us set. A person who does not lead in public prayer, who has no sensational conversion to report, and who could not teach a Sunday school class or a Bible study group, might not be considered "spiritual" in some circles; but if the sincere devotion to Jesus as Lord and Master is there, then by Paul's definition the person *is* spiritual.

Paul next makes it clear that there is only one Holy Spirit. That did not go without saying at Corinth, because in those days the Church had not realized this truth. Even the author of the Book of Revelation can speak of the *seven* spirits of God (Rev. 4:5). Paul's reason for insisting on *one* Spirit is to keep us from thinking that some "gifts" must be better, or higher, than others. It is all one and the same Spirit who works in various people with various results.

Paul does not use these words, but it is plain from what he says that the Holy Spirit is personal—no "It," no thing, but personal, though of course on a higher plane than human persons.

Paul connects the Holy Spirit with baptism, which means that to some degree all baptized persons have already known the contact of the Holy Spirit. Not that the ceremony with water produces or brings down the Spirit; on the contrary, whatever effectiveness baptism may have, comes from the Spirit himself.

The Unity of the Church as the Body of Christ (12:12-30)

At this point Paul brings in an idea which is extremely important for understanding the nature of the Church, an idea he worked out in his later letters to Ephesus and Colossae. That is the thought of the Church as a body, an organism, in which each individual Christian is a member. He had spoken to the Romans about Christians' being "one body *in* Christ" (Rom. 12:5), but now he speaks of their being "the body *of* Christ" (vs. 27).

Many thoughts arise from this one figure of speech, one of the most fruitful and suggestive in the New Testament. The main thought in this chapter, obviously, is that in the Church, as in a living body, there is *unity* and *variety*. (Note how Paul keeps his points aimed at Corinth, that split-apart church. He is not writing an essay for theologians; he is the practical pastor and bishop, saying what needs to be said to a particular congregation. And so far as we have the same diseases, we need his diagnosis and are helped by his prescription.)

There is no need for one member or organ of a body to brag of its importance. Each member of the body is useful to all the rest but in turn needs the rest. Elsewhere Paul reminds us that Christ is the Head of the Church; the Church needs him, he needs the Church. But in Corinthians the emphasis is on our need of one another. Though we all derive our true life from Christ, not one of us can live as a Christian—a living, serving Christian— without the intimate joining-with and working-with other Christians, just as it is among the members of a body. It has been suggested that we might make Paul's meaning more vivid if we translated his key phrase not "members" of one another but "membranes." To sum it up bluntly, it is no more possible to be a lone independent Christian apart from the Church than it is for an ear or an eye to be a lone independent ear or eye, with no body. An eye in a head is priceless; an eye in a glass jar is a curiosity.

Paul sums up this whole business of spiritual gifts, and puts an end to all the argument over which one is most important, in the single sentence: "To each is given the manifestation of the Spirit for the common good" (12:7).

The "More Excellent Way" of Love (12:31—13:13)

Paul does line up some "spiritual gifts" twice, in 12:8-10 and 12:27-30. Perhaps he thinks of these in order of importance, but probably not, since the two lists are not identical. The point with which he ends chapter 12 is: Desire the higher gifts; whatever gifts you feel to be higher and highest, hope and pray for these. But he goes on to mention one spiritual gift without which all other gifts are nothing, one gift in comparison with which every other is a poor second. Paul sees nothing wrong in spiritual ambition, that is, desire for great and unusual spiritual capacity and power. What he does find wrong, or tragically mistaken, is to mistake a lesser gift for the greater, or to overlook the greatest, the most essential of all.

This gift, of course, is love. The immortal 13th chapter is a prose poem on Christian love. One great Bible teacher has said that Paul probably had written this poem before this and possibly had polished it over a period of years. Then when he was writing this letter he realized that this was the very "slot" for it, so in it went. Be that as it may, this 13th chapter is one of at least four high points of this Corinthian letter. The first is 1:18—2:12, the meaning of the Cross; the second, his story of the Last Supper (11:23-26); the third, this poem on Love; and the fourth, his vision of the Christian's destiny (15:42-58). There are many shorter and unforgettable sayings, but these are longer flights if not higher.

Another writer voices this one's thought in saying that anyone who attempts to comment on this chapter of the Bible (not to mention others) comes away feeling that he has only left the mark of soiled and clumsy hands on a thing of beauty and holiness. It is a chapter that does not call for explanation so much as illustration, the kind of illustration that can be supplied only by the reader. What is true of the Bible as a whole is strongly true here: these high thoughts are meant to be lived.

Only one point will be made here, a point perhaps not realized by all readers. The Christian religion almost had to coin a new word for "love." The Greek world was not unlike our Hollywood-ized world; the word "love" had been dragged through a lot of mud. The usual word for "love" in the Greek-speaking world was a word that invariably suggested physical sex desire and not much else. (The word survives in our English word "erotic.") There was a second word several shades brighter, but still a little pale, suggesting a kind of placid friendship. What was needed was a word that would express the Christian experience of the love of God himself, the love that is outpoured even on the loveless and the unlovable, the love that sent God's Son to suffer and die with and for us. A word was needed that would be used also to refer to the attitude of Christians to one another—some word that would reflect the total un-self-seeking quality of God's love and go far beyond the always partly, sometimes wholly, selfish desire that often goes by the name of love. So, as by common consent, the writers of the books that became our New Testament took a word that was not brand-new, to be sure, but decidedly rare, a literary rather than a common word. In English letters it is *agape*, pronounced ah-gah′-pay. There is really no English word that translates it precisely. "Love" has, for many people, the taste of grease paint, the technicolor artificiality of Hollywood. It can be used for selfish, proud desire, it can be used of infatuation. *Agape* never hinted at any such things. It was a word baptized, so to speak, into Christian use. The word "charity" is just as far from a perfect translation as "love" is. The word "'charity" nowadays always suggests Lady Bountiful taking Christmas baskets to the poor. It suggests stuffing something into chinks left by imperfect justice. It suggests something patronizing. It even suggests to some people the idea of paying stone by stone for a "mansion in the sky." Love is infinitely warmer, more personal, and more permanent than what is usually meant by "'charity." Love is . . .

But why waste words? Read I Corinthians 13 over and over for yourself. Learn what love is—Christian love, God-like love. Read that chapter in all the different translations you can lay your hands on. Read it and meditate on it and let it grip your imagination and fire your soul. Read and practice it. Then you begin to know what in this world never can be fully known, the true meaning of love.

The Gift of "Tongues"; a Primitive Worship Service (14:1-40)

Paul, coming down as he always did from the sublime to the practical, now spends some time on what he calls "tongues" or "speaking in tongues." The first question is: What exactly did he mean by this? Since "tongue" is a word often used to mean "language," the obvious meaning of "tongues" here would be that it was a miraculous gift of the Spirit, by which persons were enabled to speak foreign languages that they had never learned. The principal argument to support this view is that in Acts 2, when the Christians speak in tongues these would seem to have been definite languages or at least dialects (see Acts 2); and that this "gift" at Corinth—having the same name—must be the same thing. On the other hand, if one examines what Paul says of "tongues" speaking at Corinth, one can put down the following clues:

1. It is contrasted with prophecy, that is, preaching (14:1-5).
2. *No one* understands it (vs. 2); contrast this with Acts 2:8.
3. Even the person who spoke in a tongue did not usually un-

derstand it (vs. 5), and could not interpret it himself unless the power to do so came in answer to prayer (vs. 13).

4. Speaking in a tongue is contrasted with speaking (praying or singing) with the mind (vss. 14, 19). This contrasts with speaking in any human language, for all of them come from the mind.

Considering these points, most commentators today believe that this speaking in "tongues" at Corinth—whatever may be the conclusion about Acts 2—was not the use of actual foreign tongues, but the utterance of sounds not understood by anyone. It was involuntary, no doubt. Indeed, as the reader may discover for himself, there are Christian groups today in which speaking with tongues is not uncommon. There is even one Presbyterian church in New York State where the phenomenon has occurred. This writer has talked with persons who have themselves spoken "in tongues," and has obtained some samples of what the "tongues" sound like. They are certainly no known language. Very likely these modern "tongues" are quite similar to those strange sounds in Corinth.

Paul's attitude to this sign or "gift" of the Spirit is twofold. On the one hand he agrees that tongues *are* a spiritual gift, and he thanks God he speaks in tongues more than any of them did. On the other hand, he rates this gift low when it is contrasted with "prophecy" or, as we would say, preaching. His reason for this is simple: prophecy is an expression of love, for it helps ("edifies," builds up) others; while a "tongue" only confuses the situation and does no one any good except the speaker himself.

Commentators have struggled mightily in the attempt to straighten out verses 22-25. Paul first makes a statement, then he gives an illustration; but the illustration, on the face of it, proves exactly the opposite of the statement it is supposed to illustrate! Thus:

(a) Tongues are a sign for unbelievers (vs. 22).

(b) Prophecy is a sign for believers (vs. 22).

Statement illustrating (?) *a*: If the church is filled with people speaking in tongues, an unbeliever will think they are crazy (vs. 23).

Statement illustrating (?) *b*: It is prophecy, not tongues, that convicts and convinces an unbeliever into believing that God is present in the church (vss. 24-25).

The most ingenious efforts have been not entirely successful in making sense out of this. Just one translator has boldly done what probably ought to be done, namely, reverse (a) and (b). Maybe Paul, in a rushed moment, actually dictated verse 22 as it is; or maybe a rushed secretary took down backward what Paul said correctly. At any rate, this one translator believes that what Paul meant to say in verse 22 was: Tongues are a sign not for unbelievers but for believers; while prophecy is not for believers but for unbelievers. Then the illustrations fit perfectly.

In verses 26-33 we have in a few words a picture of a Corinthian worship service, which was very likely typical of such occasions throughout the Primitive Church; and also the principles which, according to Paul, should underlie true worship in the Church. It is not said in so many words here, but we know that in Corinth, as elsewhere, for many years there was no specially constructed and dedicated house of worship. Christians would meet in any home large enough, as very small sects do today. The meeting had no program, no "order of service." All was spontaneous, unpredictable. The main feature was that everyone wanted to take part. Everyone had something to contribute. (The Greek pronoun for "each" in these verses is masculine; Paul did not mean that women did, or should, take audible part in the service.) This contribution might be a hymn (literally a psalm), a "lesson" (something he wished to teach; perhaps a Bible lesson?), a "revelation" (some special and individual truth or experience), an outburst in a "tongue," or an interpretation of the tongue. What the meeting must have been like, we can well imagine. There would have been enormous enthusiasm, but very little sense to be made out of it. Paul, with inspired common sense, points out a better way to do it. In any one meeting, not more than three persons shall be allowed to speak, and only one of these at a time. Further, unless someone is prepared to interpret the tongues, let such people be silent. Two or three "prophets" or preachers may speak, but again only one at a time. Further, the congregation (or the other prophets, it is not clear which) are not to accept just anything a prophet says; each utterance must be "weighed" and considered. Paul assumes that all (men, of course) can prophesy and should be given an opportunity to do so at some time.

We can summarize, partly in Paul's words, first the purpose of group (public) worship, and then the manner of it. Three words express the purpose: edification (building-up, vs. 26), learning (vs. 31), encouragement (vs. 31). We can apply that to our own worship services of all kinds. The main question is not, Is this beautiful, restful, "sweet"? The questions are: Does this help to build Christian character? Do we learn something about God, about the Christian life? Do we leave the service with our faith uplifted and stronger than when we came? These are the important matters. As for the manner of worship, Paul laid down no rules, only one general principle: God is not a God of confusion but of peace; therefore let all be done "decently and in order." To put all this into even shorter form: Christian public worship of God must be based on the spiritual nature of God and the spiritual need of men. Any worship that expresses the one and fulfills the other is worship God will bless.

THE RESURRECTION AND THE LIFE EVERLASTING

I Corinthians 15:1-58

The Corinthian church, we know, was made up of people who for most of their lives had belonged to other religions. All sorts of beliefs about the future life, including the belief that there is none, were represented in the background cultures of these mixed people. They would want to know: What does Christianity have to say? The Gospels had not been written, no official statement or creed had yet been adopted and published. Probably the death of loved ones had sharpened their questions.

Paul does not use the expression "immortality" till toward the end, and does not discuss the question in the form so familiar to us—the immortality of the soul. The framework of what he says is almost exclusively the resurrection of the body. This offends many modern readers, and no doubt offended Greek Christians in Corinth.

To put it very briefly, most Greeks who had any notion at all of a future existence thought of it this way: The soul is the true *self* of man. In this present life the soul is imprisoned in the body, like a living person in a tomb. At death the soul is released forever from the body and goes its way, being indestructible and immortal by nature. On the other hand, Jews who had any conception of a future life, as well as those who did not, were unable to think of the *self* apart from the *body*. For Greeks, body and soul were opposites. For Jews, body and soul were welded into the single self. A Jew would be unable to think of any future life that was not a bodily life, as this one is. Hence Jews did not think of a future life in terms of the soul, but rather of the body; and their word was always "resurrection" and not "immortality."

Paul, being a true Jew, thought as a Jew; hence his strong emphasis on resurrection. Hence also the Christian Church in the Apostles' Creed says, "I believe in the resurrection of the body," not, "I believe in the immortality of the soul." Nevertheless the Christian Church has always made room as well for the Greek belief that personality can continue in a disembodied state, or in other words, that you don't have to have a body in order to *be*. We can perhaps reconcile the two views by saying: Whether we think in terms of immortality or of resurrection, the Christian Church believes that death is not the final end of human life. "I believe in the life everlasting" can be said heartily by all of us.

But we must let Paul speak for himself and not try to make a Greek or a modern Christian out of him. Note that Paul says not a word about "heaven." People who ask about heaven, what it will be like, are thinking of our future *surroundings*. Paul wants us to concentrate on our future *selves*.

The Resurrection of Christ Is a Part of the Gospel (15:1-11)

Paul begins where he nearly always does: with the gospel which he preached. As he sums it up here, the gospel begins with the death of Christ. (The four Gospels give us a much wider view, but that is another story.) But Paul in this short summary says much more about the Resurrection than about the Cross. He emphasizes the resurrection of Christ as a fact, not a symbol, myth, legend, or some idea or vision created by faith. Christ was really raised from the dead; that is his basic fact. The story of the Cross without the story of Easter would not be the gospel.

Christ's Resurrection and the General Resurrection (15:12-19)

There were people in Corinth who could not believe in the possibility of resurrection. Paul's argument is this: Very well, suppose you are right and resurrection can never be a fact.

Then it was not a fact in the case of Jesus. And in that case who is Jesus? A dead dreamer, no conqueror of death, no divine hero, no Savior. If his resurrection is not a fact, then whatever hope we have is for this life only. Over every grave should be the motto, "All hope abandon, ye who enter here." Instead of being God's children we are pitiable fools.

Adam and Death; Christ and Life (15:20-23)

But then Paul comes back to the fact: Christ *has* been raised from the dead! One single fact will show that the alleged "impossible" is possible after all. We do not have to explain the fact, and Paul never makes any attempt to explain Christ's resurrection or ours.

Next, in one of those contrasts of which Paul was fond, he sets Adam over against Christ. As descendants of the first Adam, we are creatures marked for death. "Son of Adam" means mortal man. As descendants of the "last Adam" we are creatures marked for life. Adam stands for humanity running away from God. Christ stands for humanity restored to God. (There has been some argument here. Certainly all human beings are mortal. Does Paul mean to suggest that all human beings are destined to life, that all will be saved? In other words, does "all" in "all die" mean the same as "all" in "all be made alive"? Do both "all's" refer to the whole human race? Most commentators doubt that Paul meant this.)

The End: God Will Be All in All (15:24-28)

Paul's mind runs ahead of his train of thought here, we might say. Without setting any timetable or naming any dates, he looks into the future far beyond the general resurrection, beyond anyone's resurrection, to the final goal of destiny. Even a child can ask the question, And what happens after that? And after that and after that? Paul may have been thinking of such questions. The "end," *the* end, beyond which no one can think, is still not the windup of existence. First is *victory*, when Christ shall have destroyed everything that opposes him or is out of harmony with him. "The last enemy to be destroyed is death." What a world without death would be like, of course, we cannot even imagine. But Paul is sure that death (he almost thinks of it as personal) is a stubborn enemy of God and man, and cannot exist in the Kingdom of Christ. But Christ does not keep the Kingdom, that is, the supreme reign over all things, for himself. He delivers it to God the Father. What this means we do not fully know. What we can say is that Christ's work is never to be completed until his victory is complete, till all have been "made alive," till Christ with an eternal humility turns all his victories over to the Father of whom he had said long ago, "The Father is greater than I" (John 14:28). To ask, *"Then* what?" is peering into the mists of eternity. Is it not enough to know that in the end, God will be all in all?

An Argument from Baptizing for the Dead (15:29-34)

This is a somewhat confusing section. No one knows just what is meant. It does seem clear that some Christians in Corinth were practicing "proxy baptism," hoping that the benefits of baptism would somehow be transferred to particular persons, now dead, whom they wished to be saved. Paul does not necessarily approve of this custom, though he does not condemn it either. His argument runs: Some of you practice baptism by proxy for the dead. That shows that you already have come to some belief in a life beyond, otherwise there would be no point in your doing this.

The remainder of this paragraph contains other thoughts not connected with baptism for the dead. The first, in verses 30-32, is Paul's question: If there is no resurrection, what would be the purpose of my endangering my life by preaching? He remarks in verse 32 that if this life is all there is, then eating and drinking—that is, having a vulgar good time—is about the most we can do with it. If we must die like dogs, let us live like dogs. No doubt this was Paul's own sincere feeling; but there have been men who felt otherwise. One French philosopher said: If there is no immortality, at least let us live so that to have been deprived of it will be an injustice. Is belief in a future life a stimulus to right living? Paul finds it exceedingly important; goodness for him has little meaning unless it has the prospect of eternity before it. Moreover, the Christian should be warned that the contagion of unbelief is dangerous (vss. 33-34).

Faith's Answer to a Foolish Question (15:35-57)

The question that is asked appears in 15:35, its answer in 15:36-50. In verses 51-57 Paul's central thought is, "We shall be changed." It seems as impertinent to comment on the inspired poetic eloquence here as it was to make any remarks about chapter 13. A few prose footnotes may perhaps be usable.

Paul makes no attempt to *explain* "resurrection." There is nothing natural or inevitable about it; it is a direct act of God, a miracle.

He forestalls ancient and modern objections to the idea by making it perfectly plain that resurrection is not resuscitation. When a person has been pronounced legally and medically dead —the heart stopped and so on—and then the heart begins to beat and consciousness returns, that is resuscitation. The person gets up off the stretcher with the same body (damaged, to be sure) which he had when he was laid on it. Now resurrection, we remember, was the only category in which Paul's Jewish training would allow him to think of a future existence. But, although many persons then and now think of resurrection as resuscitation, Paul definitely did not. Suppose resurrection did mean resuscitation? It would be something to be dreaded, not hoped for. Every particle of the body is replaced every seven years or so; by the time a man is 65 he has had eight or nine bodies; who would want to get back the last one, the weak, pain-filled one, the one that gave out? But this is not the "resurrection body." The resurrection body is continuous with the present body in some way; but it is radically different, as Paul's contrasts show:

This present body (the "sown")	The resurrection body (the "raised")
perishable	imperishable
dishonored	glorious
weak	powerful
physical	spiritual
"the image of the man of dust"	"the image of the man of heaven"

What a "spiritual body"—a seeming contradiction—can be, no one knows. Perhaps Paul means a body fully suited to an immortal spirit, a body fully under control of the spirit; possibly he means a body but only in a spiritual sense.

At all events, three possibilities are ruled out by Paul. The Christian's destiny is not (a) resuscitation, nor (b) annihilation, nor (c) absorption into the Infinite. The concept of a "resurrection of the body" must mean, at least, the continuance of *personality* and *individuality*.

Two questions often asked are left on one side by Paul here as elsewhere: (1) What is the condition of those who have died but not yet been raised? Do they now exist at all? (2) What is the destiny of those who are not "in Christ"? Are all men finally to be saved? The Church has worked out rather elaborate answers to these questions, but they are not taken from Paul.

One final note: Paul's confidence about the future hope is not based on any theory of human nature; it is rooted and grounded on his faith in God. *God who raised the Lord Jesus Christ will raise us in victory with him.* Belief in immortality is not necessarily religious, not a step toward belief in God; but on the contrary, belief in God is solid enough ground for believing that he will not destroy the creatures of his love.

Imperishable Lives in a Perishing World (15:58)

Paul never stops his thought in mid-flight. He never leaves his readers high in the blue, he always comes down to a concrete runway. After all this rhapsody on the life to come, Paul suddenly comes down to an unspoken question: But what about *this* life? Is is worthless? Some Christians have thought so. Should our whole life be a "meditation on death"? Not at all: "In the Lord your labor is not in vain." Living by the light of the life to come should not paralyze us but should fill our earth-life with purpose and power.

CLOSING NOTES, GREETINGS, BENEDICTION
I Corinthians 16:1-24

The final chapter explains itself, almost. The "contribution for the saints" refers to a great project of which we hear more in II Corinthians 8 and 9: a great united act of sharing, in which the new Gentile churches were to contribute to the needs of the now famine-ridden and poverty-stricken church in Palestine. Paul asked nothing for himself, but the needs of those saints in Jerusalem were much on his mind.

Note (vs. 9) that the fact that he had enemies in Ephesus strikes Paul as a good reason for staying, not leaving!

The mention of Apollos (vs. 12) is the last we hear of this man. Paul, writing in Greek, does not say it was not *Apollos'* will to visit Corinth. He says it was not *"the* will" (literal translation)—presumably the will of God.

To the end, Paul holds up love as the guide of life. It is not a soft, easygoing love; he connects it with strength, with the qualities of a soldier (vs. 13). Indeed, verses 13 and 14 could be taken as a summary of ideal Christian character.

The "holy kiss" was the special use in the Church (among men, not between men and women) of a common form of greeting in the ancient Near East. It was later called the "kiss of peace" and was replaced by a handclasp. In this form it is used today by the Church of South India.

After dictating most of the letter Paul adds his own short paragraph in his own handwriting at the end. He puts out of the Christian fellowship, so far as he is concerned, not those with an imperfect creed but those without love for the Lord. Love is still the guide of life. Paul even sends his own love after he has pronounced the benediction.

Is this conceited? The grace of the Lord Jesus and my love be with you! On the contrary, it is a good way to end. It is easy to love our fellow men and fellow Christians, sitting in church, before the benediction; it is love *after* the benediction that counts.

THE SECOND LETTER OF PAUL TO THE

CORINTHIANS

INTRODUCTION

Who Wrote It?

As with Romans and First Corinthians, there is no question about the writer of this "second" letter to the Corinthians. It belongs to the unquestioned letters of Paul. As we said at the beginning of those other letters, there is no need to tell the story of Paul's life here. This can be learned from the Book of Acts, or from any Bible dictionary or encyclopedia. As for the character of Paul, this present letter is one of the main sources of our knowledge of the man, as we shall see.

When Was It Written?

This letter or these letters (for it is possible that we have two or more letters combined into one) were evidently written not very long after First Corinthians. If we calculate the date of First Corinthians as A.D. 56-57, then Second Corinthians would be about A.D. 57.

Why Was It Written? and How Many Letters Are There in Second Corinthians?

These two questions have to be taken up together. Paul had various purposes in writing, that is clear enough. If we conclude that more letters than one have been combined here, then we should say that Paul did not at any one time have all these reasons for writing. If we conclude that this is now and has always been only a single letter, then we should say that various parts of the letter were written for various reasons.

Let us go back over what was said about the Corinthian correspondence in introducing First Corinthians and enlarge on it a bit. The church at Corinth had been started by Paul "from scratch." He calls himself the "father" of that church (I Cor.

4:15). We cannot say that he loved these Christians more than those he had won for Christ in other cities, but so far as the New Testament shows, he certainly spent more time and thought on this church than on any other. Corinth was his problem church, as readers of First Corinthians realize.

Paul's first letter to the church at Corinth was written to warn against association with immoral "Christians." This letter is referred to in I Corinthians 5:9. (Was this letter lost?)

Later on, the Corinthian Christians wrote him a letter, which was definitely lost long since. In answer to that letter, Paul wrote a reply known to us as First Corinthians. If that letter had had the good effect Paul wanted, it might not have been necessary to write again. Paul had enough to do without writing letters, and there always had to be a good reason for his writing at all. However, the trouble at Corinth did not clear up; or, to be more precise, the troublemakers at Corinth did not shut up. So Paul paid the church a personal visit that was not at all pleasant, as we gather from his references to it. On top of that visit, Paul wrote the Corinthians again, "out of much affliction and anguish of heart" as he said in II Corinthians 2:4, a letter which made the Corinthians "sorry" and "grieved" (II Cor. 7:8). Paul both regretted writing that letter and was glad he had written it (II Cor. 7:8-9), glad, because they were "grieved into repenting." (What became of that severe letter?) Paul was so much worried about the possible effects of his letter that he sent Titus as his representative to see how things now stood in Corinth. When Titus came back, he brought such an encouraging report that Paul had to send off another letter full of thankfulness and joy. (Where is that letter?)

It used to be thought, say 300 years ago, that the letter referred to in II Corinthians 2:4 and 7:8 was our First Corinthians. Scholars are now practically unanimous in seeing that this could not be the letter Paul mentions, for it does not fit the description at all. It is now agreed on all hands that the letter we call First Corinthians and the "severe letter" were not the same.

There is agreement, then, among many interpreters that the order of the letters was (as outlined in the Introduction to First Corinthians):

1. Paul's first letter. (Where is it?)
2. The Corinthians' letter to Paul. (Lost.)
3. First Corinthians, by Paul, in answer to their letter.

4. The severe letter. (Where is it?)

5. The letter of reconciliation. (Where is it?)

What scholars do *not* agree on is the answers to the three questions. There are two lines of thought about this. The first is that:

1. Paul's first letter is entirely lost.

2. His severe letter is lost likewise.

3. The letter of reconciliation is our Second Corinthians entire. The second line of thought is that:

1. At least a fragment of Paul's first letter is in II Corinthians 6:14—7:1.

2. His severe letter is in II Corinthians, chapters 10-13.

3. The letter of reconciliation is in II Corinthians, chapters 1-9.

Which view is right? Every intelligent reader is in about as good a position to decide which of these theories is correct as any scholar could be. The arguments sum up about like this:

Those who hold the first line of thought point out:

1. This is the long-held traditional view.

2. The oldest existing manuscripts always have our Second Corinthians as one block. There is nothing to indicate a scissors-and-paste job.

3. The burden of proof must be on those who would show that Second Corinthians, as we have it, is a combination of two or three letters.

Those who hold to the second line of thought point out:

There *are* serious breaks in the stream of thought which do indicate a scissors-and-paste job. If the reader will take a careful look at II Corinthians 6:13-14, he will see a sudden change of ideas between verses 13 and 14. Verses 14-18 of chapter 6, plus verse 1 of chapter 7, fit together perfectly; but they do not fit smoothly with either 6:13 or 7:2. On the other hand, if 7:2 is read immediately after 6:13, the passage reads smoothly and sensibly.

Furthermore, there is another sharp break between chapters 9 and 10. Everything is lovely, Paul is relaxed and thankful, as chapter 9 ends. All at once the mood shifts. He is right back arguing that he is an Apostle, threatening his opponents, defending himself, obviously worried, warning the Corinthian church.

The problem boils down to this one point, really: Do these breaks in the thought of the letter, at 6:14 and 7:2 and between chapters 9 and 10, indicate that we have here several letters, or parts of letters, put together, or are these breaks no more than can be expected of a somewhat erratic writer like Paul? The reader has the right to judge this point for himself. It should be remembered that this is not a theological point at all, only a literary problem. There is no question of Paul's authorship, and no point about inspiration is involved. The only question is: Did Paul write all this letter at the same time, or did he write various parts of it at different times?

Your commentator is impressed by the sharpness of these breaks, and thinks the simplest way to account for them is to suppose that the breaks in thought are not due to slips in Paul's mind or to long interruptions while he was dictating, but are due to the fact that we have three letters from Paul fastened, so to speak, by one paper clip. Properly speaking, then, the best way to read Second Corinthians would be to read chapters 10-13 first and *then* chapters 1-9. In this commentator's opinion, 6:14—7:1 is too brief for an entire letter. If it is from another letter it is no more than a paragraph. It does, however, interrupt the thought as a whole. It sounds like a parenthesis stuck in for no special reason, if Paul wrote it as it stands.

One more point: Whatever a reader concludes about the way this "letter" was written, and whether it is a letter or letters, makes no difference at all in the value of the letter for us. The wonderful testimony of Paul's faith in 5:1-10 is not washed out in the least by supposing either that chapters 10-13 were written before chapter 5 or that they were written after it. Paul's autobiographical notes in chapters 10-13 are just as true and effective whether this is a part of the "severe letter" or not.

Special Features

Two special features of this letter (or these letters) stand out. (Hereafter we shall refer to it as "a letter" for short.)

First, it is a real *letter*, more of a letter than most of Paul's that are known to us. This is what really makes Second Corinthians so hard to read. A letter is dashed off without any outline in mind. The writer just says what comes to his mind, without trying to balance his sentences or weigh all his words. He will allude to people and happenings known to himself and the person or persons to whom he is writing, but not known to all who may be reading over his shoulder. For example: Paul speaks twice in this letter of a possible *third* visit to Corinth. When was the second? Acts tells us nothing of it, and of course there is no point in Paul's telling the Corinthians when it was, or why, because they knew. Again, Paul speaks of a "thorn in the flesh" which caused him suffering. Very likely the Corinthians knew all about this, and did not need the explanation we should like to have. So this letter is not a formal argument, carefully worked out and carried through, like Romans; it is not a series of topics one after the other, like First Corinthians. But for all that it is the most personal and self-revealing of all Paul's letters, and we may be grateful.

For this is the second special feature: it is the most autobiographical of all the letters of Paul. Now there are two kinds of autobiography, one being the kind a small boy away at camp or school writes home: On Sunday we went to church and on Monday we had a swimming meet and on Tuesday . . . and so forth. Very dull, especially when grown people try it. Much more interesting is the kind of autobiography that tells you something you couldn't see with the eye or with any camera or recording machine; the kind of autobiography that lets you into the writer's *mind*. All Paul's letters do this more or less, but this one is more intimate, more unreserved, more frank than others. Paul's weaker points come out here along with his strong ones. Paul was Luke's hero, and the picture of Paul in Acts is carefully prepared for the Christian public. As Acts tells the story, not a blemish appears in Paul's character after his conversion and only one possible error in judgment. Here in Second Corinthians we have an unretouched portrait by Paul's own hand, with features which Paul himself realizes are questionable. But we may admire him all the more for his frankness, and come at last to realize the greatness of this man. For his fight was not only with circumstances and enemies and the Devil; this man triumphed, in Christ, over himself. And this is the greatest conquest.

OUTLINE

Because of the nature of this letter, or letters, we shall not be able to make as satisfactory an outline as can be done for Romans or First Corinthians. Since the LAYMAN'S BIBLE COMMENTARY deals with every book in the order of the verses as printed in our English Bibles, we shall offer a brief outline on that plan.

Greetings. II Corinthians 1:1-2
The God of Comfort. II Corinthians 1:3-7
Paul in Trouble. II Corinthians 1:8-11
Mutual Confidence of Paul and the Corinthians. II Corinthians 1:12-14
Christ Is "Yes." II Corinthians 1:15-22
Painful Letter Versus Painful Visit. II Corinthians 1:23—2:4
Forgiveness. II Corinthians 2:5-11
Looking for Titus. II Corinthians 2:12-13
The Aroma of Christ. II Corinthians 2:14-17
Christians Are Letters from Christ. II Corinthians 3:1-3
Old Covenant and New. II Corinthians 3:4-18
The Work of the Ministry. II Corinthians 4:1—6:13

> Preaching Christ as Lord (4:1-6)
> Treasure in Earthen Vessels (4:7-12)
> All for Your Sake (4:13-15)
> A Parenthesis on Death (4:16—5:10)
> The Ministry of Reconciliation (5:11—6:13)

No Mismating with Unbelievers. II Corinthians 6:14—7:1
Titus Brings Good News. II Corinthians 7:2-16
On Christian Giving. II Corinthians 8:1—9:15
A Warning to the Disobedient. II Corinthians 10:1-6
Boasting in the Lord. II Corinthians 10:7-18
Paul's Right to Boast: His Sufferings in the Cause. II Corinthians 11:1—12:10
Paul Has Been More Than Fair. II Corinthians 12:11-18
Mend Your Ways, or Else—! II Corinthians 12:19—13:10
Farewell and Benediction. II Corinthians 13:11-14

COMMENTARY

In the commentary, each paragraph in the Revised Standard
Version will be treated as a unit. Please do not worry too much
about finding a connection of thought from paragraph to paragraph. Where that is important, it will be pointed out; but
often there will be no connection, and little use trying to invent
one.

Greetings (1:1-2)

This is a typical Pauline opening. He gives himself the familiar
and important title, "apostle of Christ Jesus by the will of
God." He names Timothy as co-author, though Timothy may
have had as little to do with writing Second Corinthians as
Sosthenes did with First Corinthians. The letter is sent not only
to Corinth but also to the Christians of Achaia, a province of the
Roman Empire, in which Corinth was an important city.

The God of Comfort (1:3-7)

Once the greeting and the signature are down on papyrus, or
whatever material he used, Paul, as is natural to him, begins with
a prayer of thanks to God. The word "bless" has at least two
meanings in the Bible. One refers to God's kind mercies to man,
as when we pray that God will bless us. It also means "praise,"
as it does here. The sentence (vs. 3) means "Praised be the God
and Father . . ." God is described in three ways: he is the God and
Father of our Lord Jesus Christ, he is the Father of mercies,
and he is the God of all comfort. These are not definitions. No
writer in the Bible ever gives a dictionary definition of God. The
Bible writers all knew God, and they no more tried to argue that
he really exists than people would argue that they are breathing
real air. There is a place and time for discussing the reality of
God, but Paul knows this is not that time and place.

Paul thinks of God as his own Father, but always first of all
God is the Father of Christ. The word "father" can easily be
misunderstood. Christian teachers in slum districts have found
that it is a little risky to use the word "father" for God,
since some children are afraid of their drunken and brutal fathers.
Paul here as always finds Christ the clue to truth. To say that

God is Father of Paul, or Peter, or the members of your church, or you, might suggest that he is most like Paul, or Peter, or some unpromising church member. No, God is most like Christ. A good deal of harm has been done by forgetting this, and by proclaiming a "God" who is really made in our own image. The true family resemblance is between God and his Son Jesus Christ.

That word "comfort" is repeated till some readers tire of it. Paul must have known he was repeating, but he did not care. He wanted that thought of God's comfort to get into his friends' minds so they could not forget it, like a tune played many times. Paul uses the word as either noun or verb not less than ten times in four sentences. He makes it plain, too, that God's comfort is not given us to be enjoyed but to be passed on.

Paul in Trouble (1:8-11)

Here we wish again that we had Paul with us to ask him what he means. What *was* that affliction in Asia? This is one of the places where his readers understood what he meant, so he does not try to make himself clearer for our benefit. This affliction might have been illness, or severe persecution, or a trial in which everything seemed to go against him. All that is clear is that Paul had been so depressed by whatever it was that he had not expected to live. When rescue came, it seemed as astounding as Christ's resurrection; it was like being raised from the dead. Paul's faith came out clearer and stronger than before; he will not give up hope the next time. John Bunyan, centuries after this, was to write some verses that included the words, "He that is down need fear no fall." Paul had been down, and now he feared no fall.

Paul believed not only in praying for himself; he wanted the help of his friends in prayer. Now that is a very remarkable thing. We know from reading First Corinthians what kind of people those Corinthians were. Say the best of them you could, they were a long distance below Paul in the Christian life. Yet this great saint and Apostle can say, "You also must help us by prayer" (vs. 11). So the weakest of Christians may help the greatest, at the throne of grace.

Mutual Confidence of Paul and the Corinthians (1:12-14)

The skeleton of verse 12 is: "Our boast is . . . the testimony of our conscience that we have behaved . . . toward you . . . with holiness and godly sincerity." This is a hint of the much larger and more elaborate "boasting" which is found in later chapters. Those who believe Second Corinthians is all one single letter, though admitting as all readers must that Paul does not stay on one track very long, nevertheless point out that the theme of boasting is found here as well as after chapter 10, and may indicate that all of Second Corinthians was written at one time. The background of Paul's anxiety to certify himself as a genuine Apostle is that his authority had been questioned by rival "apostles" not only at Corinth but everywhere he went. Verse 13 indicates that Paul thought that plain people could understand what he was saying. Verse 14 brings out an idea which is more than a "mutual admiration society"; it is a relation of confidence—Paul's confidence in the Corinthians, and theirs in him.

Christ Is "Yes" (1:15-22)

Apparently some change had been made in Paul's original plan to visit Corinth twice; and his enemies had taken this as evidence that he was wishy-washy, not knowing what he really wanted to do. This sets Paul off on his own defense: he is a Christian, he means to say, and as Christ's man he is not double-minded. He comes back to this point more than once. Just here he is reminded that Christ himself is not "Yes and No" but only "Yes." What Paul means is that you always know where Jesus stands. In small things and in great, Jesus is not—and Paul does not wish to be— of two minds. Paul does not mean that he is a "yes man"; that is the last thing he would wish to be. But he does mean to be positive, so that no one could mistake what he was standing for. The fact that he can write as he does in this paragraph about Christ and God, starting from a simple remark someone had made about him (Paul), shows how his mind is centered in God. No matter what the problem or the incident, no matter how small, Paul instinctively asks: What has this to do with Christ?

Painful Letter Versus Painful Visit (1:23—2:4)

Paul now comes back to the reason why he had not visited the Corinthian church a third time. One painful visit was enough! So, instead of another tense and unpleasant visit, he had put all the unpleasant things he had found it necessary to say into a letter.

(This was the "painful letter," and either it has been lost entirely or a good part of it is preserved in II Corinthians 10-13.)

The reason the visit was painful was that the church at Corinth was torn by quarrels and factions. Not only so, but some in the church had refused to acknowledge the authority of Paul. Just exactly what went on during that visit we do not know, but from other references as well as this one, it would appear to have been largely a matter of discipline—what to do with some person who had committed some serious sin. Who the person was and what the offense was, Paul does not say. Possibly he did say, but before these letters were released to the public, the name of the person and the details were edited out. This is just as well; at this distance personalities matter little. Paul's principles are not "dated" but are still sound.

Forgiveness (2:5-11)

From all we can tell from this letter, it seems that between the time Paul had made that painful visit, and the time he wrote, the church at Corinth had punished the offender in some way. The point here is: "Punishment by the majority is enough" (vs. 6). Paul's principles in church discipline might be stated simply:

1. There must be authority in the church with power to act.

2. All persons in the church must be subject to this authority.

3. In case of outbreaking sin, the authority must act, for the good of the church and of the sinner as well.

4. Enough is enough. Once punished, the offender should be restored by forgiveness to the fellowship of the church.

The above leaves some questions unanswered. Who, for instance, *is* the authority in the church? And what kind of punishment can a church inflict? As for Corinth, Paul undeniably looked on himself as *the* authority, as personal representative of Jesus Christ. Nevertheless, both here and in First Corinthians Paul urges the church as a whole to take action. Both democratic and nondemocratic churches point to this incident as model for the way they do things. Paul reserved the last word for himself; but he seems to have felt that if the church did its duty in sifting out evildoers, there would be little need to appeal to him. As for the penalty, it appears to have been excommunication. But here, as in I Corinthians 5:3-5 and 6:1-6, the excommunication—that is, removal from the circle of Christian fellowship—is not to be permanent. So now Paul urges forgiveness, and far from wishing to have the power to veto their action, he humbly says, "Any one whom you forgive, I also forgive" (vs. 10).

Looking for Titus (2:12-13)

Paul had not been willing to wait for a letter from Corinth telling him how things were going there. From previous experience (see I Cor.) he knew that the Corinthians were capable of writing him a long affectionate letter without ever telling him what was really wrong with the church. So he had sent Titus in his place, to see what the situation was and to report. But still he was too impatient to wait for Titus to return. Paul came as far as Troas (a visit not recorded in the Book of Acts), looking for Titus and not finding him at first. Macedonia, as Paul uses the word, generally means Philippi and other places, but especially Philippi. Paul found that church his pride and joy (Phil. 4:1), and wrote to the Philippians the happiest of all his letters. Paul had to give more thought to the church at Corinth, but we cannot say that he found the Corinthian church the most congenial.

The Aroma of Christ (2:14-17)

Now Titus did at last arrive (7:6), and the news he brought was good, but Paul does not say so here. Instead, by one of the quick shifts of thought so typical of him, he starts to praise God, presumably for the news that Titus brought, only he does not say this. He bursts into one of his elaborate by-the-way figures: the triumphal procession. To get the real picture here that Paul intended, the reader must remember that all Roman emperors were generals, and after a general had won some notable victory the Roman senate would grant him the right of a "Triumph" or victory procession. At the tail end of the procession would come those captives who, when the "Triumph" was over, would be publicly killed to top off the occasion. Paul had perhaps seen these affairs and been impressed by them. He mixes his metaphor here as he often does, but some of the main ideas are clear. Christ is the Lord of lords who celebrates his triumph. The Christians, including Paul, are the captives in the procession. We said the metaphor is mixed, because in an emperor's triumph the slaves were his enemies, and were going to be cruelly killed;

whereas in Christ's triumph the slaves are on their way to eternal life. But the point is, Christ is the victor and Christians share in his triumph over sin and death.

Another feature of this figure of speech is in Paul's reference to "fragrance." Paul may have been thinking of the incense bearers, the priests who would walk in such a triumphal procession carrying censers. To some in the procession, that perfume would always remind them of joy and peace and victory; to others, the poor men doomed to death that day, it would be an odor reminding them of the slaughter to come. So Paul, mixing his metaphor a bit more, thinks of Christians as an "aroma" or "fragrance" which, like all odors, means different things to different people. To put it in plain language: Christians should remind all men of God. But to some, God is a terror to think of; while to others he is perfect love. To some, God means *death;* to others, *life.*

Paul already has on his mind what he will develop at some length in this letter, namely, the Christian ministry. This is closely connected with the other theme on which he spends so much space, that of Paul's own credentials and authority. At the end of chapter 2, Paul in one sentence says a number of important things about the ministry. "We are not . . . peddlers of God's word," he says. A peddler cares little for what he sells; he will sell anything to make a little money. Neither does he care about the people to whom he sells. He is here today and gone tomorrow; he is interested only in making what money he can, selling anything to anybody. The true minister is no peddler; he is not in it for money, and he is keenly interested not only in what he has to "sell" but also in the people he is to reach. Further, the minister is commissioned by God; he is not self-appointed. And what he says, he says "in the sight of God," and all his speaking is "in Christ," that is, in harmony with Christ's spirit.

Christians Are Letters from Christ (3:1-3)

Paul's next thought is about his own credentials as a minister of Christ. For after all, this was forced upon him by the constant nagging of enemies and ill-wishers who kept saying that Paul was a faker, that he had no credentials. Well, of course, in the usual meaning of the word, Paul did not have credentials. He carried no diploma from any theological seminary. No one of the original

Twelve was vouching for him. He had no letters of recommendation, when he came to Corinth, from any other church. But Paul
has a happier thought. For the Corinthians, most of whom had
been converted by Paul's preaching, no credentials were needed
but just—themselves. The church might have its troubles; but
evidently there were enough real Christians there so that Paul
could point to them and say, "These people are evidence enough
to convince anyone that I am a real minister and not a faker." A
true minister writes his own record in the lives of those he has
won for God. A mother's recommendation is her children, a
teacher's is her pupils, a minister's is his people. And yet Paul
realizes that if a true Christian is a letter, the handwriting of it
is no man's but is God's. So he speaks of the letter as being "from
Christ" and written "with the Spirit of the living God."

Old Covenant and New (3:4-18)

This thought leads Paul to reflect on something else written
by God, the Ten Commandments. Perhaps Paul did not think of
God as literally writing or carving the Ten Commandments on
slabs of rock, any more than he thought of the Holy Spirit as
literally inscribing words on a person's heart. But as a figure of
speech it is a powerful one. Being a Jew, Paul had given a great
deal of thought to the relation and the difference between the
religion of the Jews and the religion of Christ. Readers of Romans will recall the long chapters he devotes to this thought. You
might almost say this problem was never far from his mind.

The modern reader is inclined to skip all this as unimportant,
something dragged in. So he skips all the chapters in the New
Testament that reflect on the relation between Judaism and Christianity. This, however, is to miss something of value. It is no
doubt true that only a Jewish reader can feel the full force of
Paul's remarks in such chapters as Romans 4, 9, 10, 11, and II
Corinthians 3. But even a non-Jewish reader can translate this,
so to speak, into more universal terms. Remembering that Judaism was beyond question the highest form of religion the world
had then seen, we can say at least this: that if Christianity
is seen to be superior after comparison with Judaism, it will certainly not be the loser in comparison with any other religion.

Consider the contrasts as Paul brings them out here. First
(3:4-6), both the old religion and the new are *covenant* religions;
that is, the basic idea in both is a two-way relation between

God and man. In theologians' language, covenant religion is one of revelation and response; God speaks and man replies. Neither religion is one of "climbing the altar stairs"; each one teaches that God first comes to man, not man to God. But the Old Covenant, Paul suggests, is in a written code, while the New Covenant is in the Spirit. The written code kills, but the Spirit gives life. Christian life cannot be reduced to a code or expressed by rigid law.

In 3:7-8 Paul speaks of the "dispensation of death" and contrasts it with the dispensation of the Spirit. Paul is not speaking as a dissatisfied Jew, but as one who in the old days was fiercely loyal to the Law. Yet we have his testimony (as for instance in Romans 7) that the Law had simply not brought him life. The least you could say was that so far as he was concerned, the difference between his old faith and his new faith was like the difference between death and life.

In 3:9-10 the contrast is between condemnation and righteousness. To get the background of what Paul is saying here in very short fashion, one could read the first five chapters of Romans. The main point right here is that a religion of law, even (and especially) God's Law, succeeds only in giving a sense of frustration and guilt. The religion of Christ brings the righteousness which is "through faith," as Paul would put it. Again, the Old Covenant is temporary, the new one permanent; and so, while both are "religions of splendor" (as indeed all are to some degree), the New Covenant alone has a splendor which will not fade away.

Paul goes further still in his contrasts (3:12-16). The Old Covenant and the New had, in Paul's time, exactly the same Scriptures. None of the New Testament had yet been placed by the Church on a par with the Old Testament, and most of the New Testament had not in fact been written. Whether you attended a synagogue or a Christian meeting you would hear exactly the same Scriptures being read. But in the synagogue "whenever Moses is read a veil lies over their minds." We do not know all that Paul meant by this, but we can guess with good reason that he was thinking how much of the Old Testament points to Christ but that *only the Christian can see this*. That is to say, for example, that when a Christian reads Isaiah 53 he can read it as a portrait of Christ, while outside of the Christian faith that chapter remains a rather dark puzzle.

Two more contrasts are suggested rather than worked out in full (3:17-18). The New Covenant, unlike the Old, is one of *freedom*. In Paul's own thought, he had been a slave to the Law; now he has been set free by Christ (see Gal. 5:1). Again, the believer under the Old Covenant had his eye fixed, so to speak, on certain written laws. The believer under the New Covenant fixes his eye on a Person. Note the phrases, "through Christ" (vs. 14), "turns to the Lord" (vs. 16), "where the Spirit of the Lord is" (vs. 17), "beholding the glory of the Lord" (vs. 18). There is all the difference in the world between the struggle to fulfill precisely a set of laws, and being so captured by the Spirit of Christ as to be transformed "into his likeness" (vs. 18).

The Work of the Ministry (4:1—6:13)

The longest single passage in Second Corinthians with one over-all theme is this on the ministry. Here is the essence of what it means to be a minister of the gospel, of the "new covenant" (3:6), or "the ministry of reconciliation" (5:18). Indeed, we can think of this section as beginning with 2:17, where Paul speaks of "peddlers" as contrasted with those who are "commissioned by God." If we think of the section on the ministry as beginning there, we can say now (at the start of chapter 4) that he has already spoken of the minister's commission, of his true recommendation, and of the glory of the New Covenant which he proclaims and in which he stands.

Now Paul begins more plainly to speak of what it means to be a Christian minister. Laymen may think this is only for preachers, and skip it; but Paul is not writing to preachers. He is writing about preachers to people who were *not* professional preachers. You cannot afford to skip this, if you are a Christian. What kind of church would we have if only the ministers knew what they were trying to do? Indeed, that is just what is wrong with some churches—the minister is almost alone in knowing what his real work and aims are. Pulpit committees will call men who turn out to be failures because the committee and the congregation in selecting and calling them ask the wrong questions.

Preaching Christ as Lord (4:1-6)

Paul admits that the ministry is at times a discouraging business (4:1), but he refuses to be downhearted. The minister first of all speaks the truth openly, the truth about God and about man. This may or may not be what people want to hear; but if the minister is muzzled, if he cannot or is afraid to speak his own conviction, he is no true minister. Paul faces the fact (4:3-4) that some people will not hear the truth, nor see it. "The god of this world" (probably meaning Satan) blinds the eyes of some, so that they cannot see the light even when it is shining into their eyes. But the light is there; the light is Christ.

Paul says "we" all the time he is writing of the ministry. Perhaps he just means himself; or perhaps he means himself and all true ministers. At all events the genuine minister does not preach (talk about, praise, recommend, proclaim) himself. The best sermons do not leave as strong an impression of the preacher as they do of Christ. "We preach . . . Jesus Christ as Lord" (4:5). It is a mistake, or at least it is out of line with Paul's ideal, to proclaim Christ as Savior but nothing more. People can accept him as Savior, happily sing "Jesus paid it all," and proceed on their same stupid, sinful ways, very little changed. If Jesus is proclaimed as *Lord*—that is, with supreme authority for faith and life—we cannot take him as such and stay the way we were. And of course the reason Christ must be Lord is that he is "the likeness of God" (4:4). Paul has many ways of describing the change to being a Christian from not being one. Here it is as light shining into darkness. Christian life does not begin with something we do or accomplish; it begins with God shining into our hearts, but the light comes from the face of Jesus Christ.

Further, Paul cannot split preaching off from service. A sick person gets a diagnosis from a doctor, and a prescription too. This will not get the patient well. There has to be a great deal of *service* by doctor, nurse, and others. So the minister's work is not all proclamation or preaching. It is not all diagnosis and prescription. Ministers are "your servants for Jesus' sake"; that is it in a nutshell.

Treasure in Earthen Vessels (4:7-12)

The gospel of Christ is always better than any preacher. Paul feels as if he were a cheap crockery jar containing a hoard of jewels. The minister is like a very frail wire carrying a vital message. But if the message comes through it does not matter how frail the wire may be. Life and death were mingled in Paul's experience. He was literally never far from death, yet his very weakness shows that "the . . . power belongs to God" and not to his own strength or genius.

All for Your Sake (4:13-15)

Here we come to one of Paul's typical transitions, showing how his mind worked and where it was centered. He intertwines two thoughts in this short paragraph: (1) All that he does and suffers is for the sake of others; and (2) he is sure that as he shares the sacrificial suffering of Christ he will share also in Christ's resurrection. (This is not a lone offhand surmise on his part; it was central in his thinking. See Colossians 3, where he later worked out this theme of rising with Christ and applied it to this world rather than the next.) Now the thought of the Resurrection leads him on to speak of death and what comes after it, so, for the moment, he drops the theme of the Christian ministry.

A Parenthesis on Death (4:16—5:10)

This is a real parenthesis, because 5:11 fits very nicely to 4:15; but, like Paul's side remarks in general, it lets us in to some vital truths. You might put it this way: Paul is saying, "I know that I am in constant danger and am wearing myself out working so hard; my life may be short and death only around the corner. *But so what?* Death will not destroy me; it will only bring me closer to the Lord." Physically, Paul is growing every day older and weaker, and yet inwardly, spiritually, he keeps forever young. In 4:7-10 and 11:23-29 Paul speaks of the very great hardships he had suffered, but here he dismisses all of this lightly as a "slight momentary affliction" (4:17). It is all a preparation for an "eternal weight of glory"; that is, glory so great that one cannot bear the thought of it. This word "glory" is one Paul often uses to describe the Christian's next life. It is an indefinite word, used on purpose, because our minds are not capable of imagining what God has in store for us (see I Cor. 15:43; Rom. 8:18; 9:23; Col. 1:27; 3:4).

The things which are unseen are eternal (4:16-18). Death is dismal only if you think that nothing is real except what you can see and touch and hear. Death, physically, means decay, destruction. The great dividing line between religion—any religion and not only Christianity—and no-religion is right here: Can what is neither seen nor heard nor felt be real? Are all realities only those we can measure with some kind of scales or yardstick? The person who is a materialist—that is, one who believes that all that is real can always be seen, touched, and measured—can think of death only as the great destroyer. A person who believes only in the "natural" cannot see beyond death—not an inch; only believers in the *super*natural (that is, in reality that no laboratory can ever discover or measure) can believe in life beyond this life.

Paul compares the difference between this life and the next (remember he is speaking for himself and other Christians) to the difference between living in a tent and in a house (5:1-5). The tent is temporary; it is temporary on purpose. It is made to be portable. But a house is built to last. To be sure this is an imperfect illustration, for even a house wears out in time, and Paul does not mean that the next life, like this one, finally ends in decay! Still, just as most people would much rather live in a house than in a tent, so the next life is actually more *livable* than this one. Here we are camping out; yonder we shall be at home. Paul made tents and sold them, and he knew what he was talking about. A man who lives in a tent never belongs where he is; he belongs somewhere else. A man in a house belongs there. So death is not a leaving home; it is a going home. We could ask no finer words for the next life than Paul's immortal phrase, "so that what is mortal may be swallowed up by life." (Isn't that the exact opposite of what irreligious people think? They suppose that in death, life has been swallowed up by destruction!)

There are two kinds of courage in the face of death. One is the courage of despair, the other the courage of hope (5:6-10). Paul expresses the second: "We would rather be away from the body and at home with the Lord." Paul does not even consider the possibility of not *being*. Philosophers and others who talk about Christian courage as if it were calmness in the prospect of "non-being," are talking about the courage of despair, not of hope. For Paul, the truth is that now I am, and then (beyond death) I shall be. The difference which death makes is not between being and not-being; it is a difference between being in a tent and being in a house, being away from home and being at home, being away from the Lord and being with him.

Paul does not ever go into much detail about the next life, and we may well believe his silence was inspired. Yet one feature of that life he often mentions: the Judgment. Two points in verse

10 should be noted. One is that Christ is the Judge; this is one of the notable ways in which Paul ascribes to Christ a final and absolute authority equal to that of God. If we could say so reverently, when Paul draws a picture of either this life or the next, in the place where we expect to find a blank space for the invisible God (Paul's own word, Col. 1:15), we see the Lord Jesus. The other feature of verse 10 is that here Paul seems to teach that human destiny depends on what we do, good or evil. There are people who believe that this is what Paul meant. Others, including most Protestants, know that when Paul set out to discuss this very question, On what does a man's final destiny depend? his answer can be summed up (as all readers of Romans know): Not on actions but on faith; it is not what man does but the grace of God that saves him. So here Paul is not contradicting himself. What he most likely means is that not justification but *rewards* are given in accordance with what men have done of good or evil. In other words—if you want to push this further— there are grades of joy and blessedness in heaven, and grades of horror in hell.

The Ministry of Reconciliation (5:11—6:13)

Paul now comes back from the Last Judgment to his main theme in this part of his letter, namely, the work of the Christian ministry. In 5:11 he uses one of his all-embracing phrases: "Knowing the fear of the Lord [he means reverence, not fright], we persuade men." The minister stands between God and men; it is only as he knows God that he can persuade men. It is not Paul who gives Paul dignity, but God. Paul does not commend himself; he commends Christ. He may have been accused of being off-beat, off-center. Well, he says, if he has been crazy it is for God's cause. Paul, like all true preachers ever since, however sensational he might be, had as his root-motive nothing selfish, much less crazy. "The love of Christ controls us," he says. He means first of all the love Christ had shown to him, but possibly he means also the love he has toward Christ. The Christian reader should stop and think about this sentence a long time. What *is* my motive in Christian work? What should be a young man's reasons for entering the ministry, a girl's for becoming a deaconess or a missionary? It is much better not to be a minister at all than to be one for the wrong reasons.

"One has died for all." Here as in many places Paul starts

from the Cross to find the meaning of Christianity. Verses 14 and 15 are a summing up of the whole Christian life. There is an argument about these verses. Does Paul mean by "all," all men, or only all for whom Christ died? Can you go to *any* human being *anywhere* and say, "Christ died for *you*"? Some theologians do not believe that Paul could have meant what he says here. But if we go on the principle that it is best to understand Paul (or anyone else) on the basis of his clearest and plainest statement on any topic, then it is hard to see where Paul ever expressed himself more flatly and unmistakably than here: Christ died for *all*. There are churches that teach that God has no intention or wish to save some people; but the majority of Christian churches teach that, in Paul's words, God "desires all men to be saved" (I Tim. 2:4). This does not mean that all *will* be saved; God leaves men free even to say No to him, No to the Christ on the cross.

Verse 16 does not mean that Paul had a sort of out-of-this-world attitude to other people. It is another side of what we have already noticed: What is real is always more than meets the eye. He has been talking about salvation, only calling it not "salvation" but "life," and in verse 17 he comes to this point: What happens to a man when he is converted? Outwardly, nothing at all. He has been to church, he has been impressed by sermon or prayer or hymn, he consciously gave his heart to the Lord. And he goes home to Sunday dinner as usual. But Paul says he is a "new creation." What he means is that if you look at the man as, say, the policeman or his boss looks at him, "from a human point of view," he is still plain John Doe. But as God sees him, something has happened to him, inside. A new creation has begun, a new life has started. Paul does not use the words "new birth," but "new creation" is just as radical and means the same. Paul telescopes the life experience of a Christian; he says the old has passed away, the new *has come*—not fully come, as he well knew from those half-baked Corinthians, but the start has been made.

The life in Christ, furthermore, is not something a man simply decides to do, not a mere turning over a new leaf. It is something God does to and in a person. And yet there is no getting away from personal response, taking or rejecting God's love in Christ. Paul does not say, "All this is from God and therefore you don't need to do a thing." He says, "All this is from God

. . . So we . . . beseech you on behalf of Christ, be reconciled to God" (5:18-20).

Here as elsewhere, Paul speaks of our being reconciled to God, not of his being reconciled to us. Other religions may recommend ways of persuading the gods to be gracious. The Christian religion knows that the only God is a God of grace. He does not need to be won over to us; we need to be won over to him.

Here again it is well to stop and think as deeply as you can into this profound truth. What does it mean to be an enemy of God? How do we show hostility to him? Why is being reconciled to God the same thing as becoming a "new creation"?

And again Paul reminds us of the terrible yet triumphant paradox—the truth that is too strange to seem true—that, so to speak, God came so far over on our side that in Christ he not only became human, joining the human race, but he took the place of the human sinner. Christ knew no sin, yet he was *made to be sin*. As he took our place he gave us his. Paul has already (I Cor. 1:30) called Christ our righteousness; here he calls us the "righteousness of God in him [Christ]" (see 5:21).

Verse 21 can be called the whole doctrine of the Atonement in a single sentence. If someone complains that Paul does not fully explain it, all we can say is, How can anyone *explain* the love of a God who identifies himself with his own enemies in order to re-create them as his friends? It is really a good thing that God does not always act "rationally" toward us. If he did, we could have small hope. The God who is love does the unexpected, the unexpectable. We have to remember that when the God of love walked this earth as a man, some people thought him crazy and some thought him bad. A God who does nothing but what respectable citizens will approve would be a sorry sort of God.

Nevertheless, salvation—the new life in God—is not simply God's affair. It does not come automatically, without our knowledge and consent. If Paul had thought so he never would have gone on (6:1) to say, "We *entreat* you . . ." There is no point in the Christian life, at its beginning or in the midst of it, at which God does it all. Always we are called on to respond. The people at Corinth were Christians, church members. Paul is not appealing to them to accept Christ; they had done that. What he fears is that they have accepted God's grace in vain; that is, they have gone on living as if God had never come in Christ to their rescue.

Paul now (6:3-13) rather suddenly comes back to the main theme of this section, the nature of the Christian ministry. He has been speaking about the message of the minister, the plea for *harmony with God* which as we have said is one of the main themes of the epistle. Now he speaks of the minister—of himself in particular, as the minister he knew best. Again we find a passage calling for meditation rather than explanation. Up to verse 9 it is clear enough. The point is: Does it resemble the reader's own experience? What Paul says can be applied to all forms of Christian service. Isn't it true that most of us serve God—when we do—for selfish reasons? Isn't it true that we serve him when convenient, and not otherwise? How many young men would turn back from the ministry if they knew that what Paul describes in verses 4-8 would be their lot? How many of us refuse to serve just as soon as it becomes a little bothersome?

The long sentence beginning in verse 8 is not merely an example of Paul's paradoxical style. It is the double truth about the Christian ministry. The truth is so double that it can be described only by what sounds like double talk. Ask Paul: What do you get out of being a missionary? He could honestly say, "What do you think? People claim I'm a faker; I have no reputation to speak of; I have to live in the slums; I'm often within inches of death; I get stiff sentences in the courts; I could sit down and cry—and I do—over these 'Christians' and their stupid sins; I barely make ends meet, in fact they don't meet." But Paul could also say honestly: "What do I get out of it? Everything! It isn't only that I'm known from Jerusalem to Rome; God knows me and that's enough. The nearer I am to death, the nearer I am to the life everlasting. I haven't been killed yet, though a good many have tried it. I have learned to find joy in all that I do. I may not have money, but I have brought to many what money cannot buy, and they are grateful. I have everything God wants me to have, and that's enough for any man."

No Mismating with Unbelievers (6:14—7:1)

In verses 11-13 Paul begins a plea for harmony between himself and the Corinthians. His heart is open to them; let theirs be just as open to him. But he barely gets started on this line when (as our Bibles print it) he interrupts himself to speak of something entirely different in verses 6:14—7:1. We have seen (see Introduction) that a number of interpreters believe this section is actually a part of the letter to which Paul refers in I Corinthians 5:9. Be that as it may, it does not fit either what goes before or what comes after, in spite of great efforts on the part of commentators to make it appear to do so. In any case, we shall take a look at it here, since we are following the text of the letter as it has come down to us.

The main meaning is clear enough: "Do not be mismated with unbelievers." This is the same advice to which Paul refers in I Corinthians 5:9, if not a quotation from the same letter. Paul explains what he means by this, in I Corinthians 5:9-11. He does not mean that Christians are never to have any dealings with non-Christians. He does mean that Christians ought not to have unbelievers in the church membership. This is a warning against accepting hypocrites as if they were genuine Christians. Now the unbelievers of whom Paul speaks are not people with some off-beat ideas; they are not imperfect Christians (otherwise we should all have to be shut out of the Church). They are (as described in I Cor. 5) immoral, idol-worshipers, robbers, and so on; in II Corinthians 6 such words are used as "unbeliever," "iniquity," "darkness." The Scripture Paul quotes is taken from various books of the Old Testament; the central point, verse 17, is from Isaiah 52:11 and refers to outright pagans, the people of Babylon.

People who rely on this passage to justify leaving a Christian church are misusing it. They read it as if it said: "Do not be mismated with people who do not believe precisely as you do." This is not Paul's meaning. What he is pleading for is a Christian Church made of *Christians;* not—even partly—of people who are indifferent or opposed to Christ and his cause and his people. It is also a warning against trying to combine the Christian Church with other religions. Christianity can be itself only when it is not mixed with other faiths. When a man becomes a Christian he is asked to leave his idols at the door.

Titus Brings Good News (7:2-16)

The short passage, 6:11-13 and 7:2-4, interrupted by the longer section 6:14—7:1, brings to a temporary climax the letter we have been reading. We say "temporary climax" because it is very like Paul to come up to a climax, as a great symphony rises to a finale, and then begin all over again perhaps on another theme. (Other examples are Romans 8 followed by chapter 9; I Corinthians 15 followed by chapter 16.) Paul has been speaking off and on about the relations between himself and the Corinthian Christians. Now he makes it clear that if there is any rift, any cloud, about that relationship, it is in their hearts, not his. No one could make a stronger statement than he makes in these verses. They are in his heart (his and Timothy's) to live and die together; he is proud of them; he is overjoyed.

The rest of chapter 7 is all centered in the arrival of Titus with good news. Paul started to speak of this in 2:12-13, and now returns to the point. After a time of disappointment, when he could not locate or communicate with Titus, that man at last arrived; Paul does not say when or where. But the same overwhelming joy which Paul describes in the early verses of the chapter, shines through all of it. We can see that he had at one time wished he had not written that "severe letter." Paul himself would one day write, "Fathers, do not provoke your children to anger" (Eph. 6:4); he might well have felt that he had made his letter too strong, so that all the Corinthians might break out in open revolt against him. But now Paul sees that his regret was needless. He points out to the Corinthians all the good which his letter had accomplished. They were shocked into a good frame of mind and spirit; they had acted vigorously in the case of the offending church member. Paul feels that the whole case has come out in a personal vindication for himself, and this seems to be his main reason for rejoicing in the incident.

It is said that when Oliver Cromwell sat for his portrait he insisted that all his warts be plainly shown in the picture. We do not admire the warts, but we do admire the man who was candid about them. So we have said that this letter of Paul's reveals some character traits which Luke never brings out. Here, for example, we have a man obviously oversensitive, highly emotional, bragging before he was sure of his facts, distinctly self-assertive. He even admits, among friends, that his motive in writing the letter mainly had to do with none of the figures in the unpleasant incident (which is never definitely described), but with his wish to have the Corinthians realize how strong they were for Paul (7:12).

These features present Paul as a man it would not have been entirely easy to live with. And yet, as with Cromwell's warts, we cannot help admiring the man for his frankness. The complete sincerity of this intense man, the way he raises the blinds, so to speak, and invites us to look right into his heart, disarms our criticisms. After all, what would a milder man have made of the situation at Corinth? The mess there, which is always left a little shadowy in all the correspondence, called for severe measures and immediate action; Paul was there with what it took. Yet he was wise enough to realize that if he went in person, his own explosiveness might touch off some fatal fireworks. So he let the gentler Titus be the go-between. And it worked.

But Paul knows whom to thank: not himself, not Titus, not the Corinthians, but God who had wrought in their hearts.

On Christian Giving (8:1—9:15)

The next two chapters, 8 and 9, have been thought by some to be a letter, or even two letters, in themselves. The only good reason for supposing this to be true is that they are on a separate subject from the rest of the letter. A survey of Paul's letters would show that this is not unusual with him. We should note that while there is a shift in subject, there is no shift in atmosphere. The same relaxed assurance with which he has been writing carries right on into these "financial" chapters. So there is really no good reason for supposing that there has been any editorial scotch-taping at this point. Paul does repeat himself somewhat, but this was a habit with him, one might almost say a trademark.

There is almost no need for a commentary on these chapters, so far as difficulties go. There are really only two small points that may seem obscure. One is the question: Who are the men mentioned in 8:18 and 22? Nobody knows. Many have thought the unknown "brother" of verse 18 is Luke, but that is no better than a guess. Since Paul at this point is trying to arouse confidence in the way the fund he speaks of is going to be handled, you would expect him to name, as well as describe, all the committee in charge. But he does not. In verse 23 the Greek word translated "messengers" is actually "apostles." This is one of the places where it appears that in the Early Church the word "apostle" was not confined to the original Apostles.

What fund is this? Paul is not talking about Christian giving in general, but about a particular project he had started. Before he gets through with it, again typically, he has launched into some great thoughts on giving in general. But this is *"the* offering" he is talking about. Besides being preacher, organizer, theologian, bishop, writer, and poet, Paul was a man of business. He was a "fund-raiser" as we would call him today, a shrewd and practical man who knew how to go after money and get it.

This particular fund is mentioned in Romans 15:25-28, also in I Corinthians 16:1-4. (First Corinthians was, of course, written before this, and Romans a few years after this.) You should refresh your mind on those other passages before you read II Corinthians 8 and 9.

The church at Jerusalem, as readers of Acts will remember, experimented with property and practically abolished private property. "No one said that any of the things which he possessed was his own, but they had everything in common" (Acts 4:32). From the common fund, thus created, the committee headed by Stephen distributed "to each as any had need" (Acts 4:35). This was a successful plan for a while. The author of Acts says, "There was not a needy person among them" (Acts 4:34). But by the time Paul wrote Second Corinthians, some twenty years later or more, the mother church at Jerusalem had fallen on evil days. The cause was partly a famine, which of course they could not help. But their poverty was also due to the fact that in their generous sharing of what they had, they forgot something important: production. Their system of distribution worked splendidly; but distribution without production ends in the poorhouse, for individual or nation. You reach the point where your system of distribution has nothing left to distribute.

At this low point in the Jerusalem community's history, Paul conceived a simple but hopeful plan. Jerusalem was the mother of all churches; why not let the children come to their mother's rescue? It is this fund-raising scheme that is the subject of II Corinthians 8 and 9, as well as of the passages in Romans and First Corinthians already mentioned. But its real importance to us is that in dealing with this particular fund, Paul brings out a great deal that is universally true. This section has been well called "A Philosophy of Christian Giving."

At the risk of making wooden and artificial what is actually smooth-flowing and alive, we shall not try any paragraph-by-paragraph notations but shall sum up these two chapters under various heads, under the main title, "How to Raise Money in the Christian Church."

First, we note several *general principles.*

(1) *Consecration.* "First they gave *themselves* to the Lord" (8:5), Paul says of certain Christians whose generosity had surprised him. Without consecration each contributor opposes himself, for without consecration a man will give, no matter how good the cause may be, only what he can spare out of what he plans to spend on himself. Without consecration, a giver will think, "What can I get by with?" This is why giving, as the Christian Church encourages it, is a means of grace. In order to meet the challenge of some benevolence fund, there has to be a spiritual revival first. Giving, to put it plainly, is a part of the committed Christian life. This is why raising money for Christian purposes by means of raffles, carnivals, and the like is unchristian. Money thus spent by a man at a gambling device is virtually stolen from the man by the church. Money taken in by selling in a "bazaar" goods for three times the normal value is likewise stolen. Funds for Christian purposes should be given by Christian people as part and token of their personal devotion to the Lord, not raised in ways that contradict the spirit of Christ.

(2) *Readiness,* that is, willingness, the spirit of the cheerful giver. By the way, the word translated "cheerful" (9:7) means more than an absence of grumbling. It borders on the meaning "gay," and is in fact the root of our English word "hilarious." Paul does not want reluctant or forced contributions. There were to be no assessments in the Corinthian church. He does not mention any sum which the church should supply as its quota, or any average per member, or any minimum amount. He says not a word about tithes. He wants free gifts from those who are consecrated to the Lord. When the consecration and the willingness are there, you do not need to worry about quotas.

(3) *Proportionality.* Maybe that is too long a word. But there is no short one to express this third principle of Christian giving. "If the readiness is there, it is acceptable *according to what a man has,* not according to what he has not" (8:12). Paul does not want the Corinthians to be too generous. Is it possible for Christians to be too generous? Can any virtue be overdone? Yes, indeed! Granted, more people are too stingy rather than too free with their gifts. But an overgenerous giver will reduce himself

to the point where he in turn needs help, and this Paul does not want.

(4) *A Definite Purpose*. (This may belong under the head of "method," but it is a principle as well.) Paul does not encourage the Corinthians to give, he just encourages them to giving. He does not cover up what he wants to do with the money by some big word like "benevolences." He had already explained (in First Corinthians) where this money was going. Churches that leave a basket at the door for "Missions" never take up anything like as much as churches that invite missionaries to visit them and tell of particular needs in particular places.

Second, in these chapters there are suggested several *methods*.

(1) *Someone to Push*. Everybody's business is nobody's business. Some person, some group in the church, has to have the special responsibility of fund-raising. Paul in this case was the pusher. Churches nowadays use, sometimes, firms of professional fund-raisers. This is not bad, provided such firms do not resort to non-Christian devices to pry money loose from the unwilling. Further, the professionals are not likely to touch a job if they have no one to work with and are expected to do it alone.

(2) *Honesty*. Paul aims at "what is honorable not only in the Lord's sight but also in the sight of men" (8:21). Honesty is required not only in stating the aims in view, but also in accounting to the givers for what has been spent. Church budgets and treasurers' reports, dry as they may seem, are the church's way of carrying out the basic principle of honesty in church finance. Modern banking and business methods were then unknown. The funds raised in Achaia (including Corinth) and Macedonia (including Philippi, Thessalonica, and Beroea) would have to be taken to Jerusalem in cash, by personal messenger. Paul was of course scrupulously honest, and he knew that his own churches knew it. But he had enemies, and to keep those enemies from being able to cast the least shadow of suspicion on him, Paul proposed that the funds be conveyed not by himself alone but by a committee. He names some of this committee in 8:16-24, and gives the qualifications of them all. This is the equivalent of our modern audit. It is no reflection on a treasurer, or on a finance committee, to have their accounts audited. It is a temptation to say, "This is the Lord's work, we are accountable to God alone, we do not need to be approved by men"; but that is the way men talk when they are about to juggle the accounts. A good

treasurer, a good committee dealing with money, will not only welcome an audit, they will insist on it.

(3) *Psychological Smartness*. Once in a while you hear someone say that for success we ought not to depend on psychology but on the Holy Spirit, especially in the work of the Church. Paul did not feel that way about it. He did depend on the Holy Spirit; he used psychology, too. For psychology is just a word for the way people *tick*, the way their minds work, the motives that affect them, and so on. If you find a door locked, you do not try to open it by whistling into the keyhole. You use a key, because it is the nature of locks to respond to keys, not whistles. That's all psychology is: knowing what keys to use to get into people's minds.

One bit of psychology Paul uses is something close to flattery. He tells the Corinthians (8:7) that they excel in everything—in faith, knowledge, and love, for example; and urges them to bring their generosity up to the level of their other virtues. This does not sound like the Corinthians described in Paul's earlier letter to them. Paul could condemn the Corinthians, or the Galatians, or any church to which he was writing; and often he did so. But when you are raising money it is no time to find fault. If 8:7 is an exaggeration, it is a pardonable one under the circumstances.

Yet is it an exaggeration from Paul's point of view? The good news about the church at Corinth, which he had received from Titus, filled him with such comfort and delight (see ch. 7) that he very likely, at that time, could see no fault in the Corinthians. The last sentence before he begins speaking of the offering for Jerusalem ends, "because I have perfect confidence in you."

Another psychological move on Paul's part is the way he played off Corinth and Philippi (or Achaia and Macedonia) against each other. He brags about Achaia to Macedonia (9:2-4) and about Macedonia to Achaia (8:1-5). Those two provinces of the Roman Empire had once been rival states in Greece. Old rivalries die slowly, and Paul makes use of this one. He knew that a church in Achaia would not willingly let a church in Macedonia outdo it, and vice versa. Some would call this a moral compromise; but it seems better to let human nature work with you than against you.

(4) Perhaps another point of method is suggested in 8:7, namely, *persistence*. Many a good work has never been more than an intention, because once the first enthusiasm was over, nobody

had the patience to carry on and on. "Whatever is worth doing is worth doing well," the proverb says; and likewise, whatever is worth doing is worth carrying through to the finish. A distinguished business executive has said that in his office the word "practically" is forbidden; for when someone reports that a job is "practically" done it means all done but the most difficult parts of it. Many a church fund-raising campaign has gone on the rocks because by the time it was "practically" done everybody quit, and it was never done after all.

Third, Paul appeals to at least three *motives,* and their high spiritual nature indicates the really high regard he must have had for the Corinthian church. An unspiritual church would hardly rise to such motives as these.

(1) Giving is *a test of love* (8:24, and by implication all the way through). Christian giving is a way of putting I Corinthians 13 into action.

(2) Giving by Christians is *modeled after the self-giving of Christ.* The real measure of Christian generosity is not what some church somewhere else has done, but what Christ has done. Christian "giving" which denies in any way the spirit of Christ cannot really be called Christian.

(3) Christian giving produces profound *spiritual results.* Paul is a practical man and he does not overlook two quite practical points: This gift to Jerusalem will keep some fellow Christians from going hungry, and also some day they may come to your rescue if you are in the same kind of trouble. But Paul does not stop with this. Note the climax to which he rises at the end of chapter 9. This service will not only supply the wants of the saints but will overflow in many thanksgivings to God. This gift will glorify God; it will be a public testimony to the gospel's truth and power; and it will be a source of grace within the givers themselves. Thus Christian giving is not only a part of Christian living; it is also a means and support of the life in Christ. Plain ordinary money can be a seed out of which grow the finest fruits of the Spirit.

A Warning to the Disobedient (10:1-6)

With chapter 10 we come to the final section of Second Corinthians, mostly about Paul himself. We have already noted the fact that most contemporary interpreters see this section as a separate letter—indeed, probably the "severe letter" which he was both sorry and glad (7:8) he had sent. A reader need not worry his head over this if he does not wish to or is not interested. But if he *is* interested, the problem is one every reader knows as much about as a commentator does. All the data, all the clues, are in plain sight. To repeat what was said earlier: Is the break between these last four chapters and the preceding chapters sharp enough so that you cannot believe that a man in his senses would have been likely to follow chapters 1-9 with chapters 10-13? We have good evidence that not only in the Bible but also in other ancient literature some documents as we have them today are certainly not the documents in the order as written (Jeremiah is a case in point). Is Second Corinthians another case in point?

There can be no *proof* here one way or the other. The present commentator can only record his own impression: namely, that the more he looks at it, the less chapters 10-13 sound as if they could have been written after chapters 1-9 and sent off at the same time. In their present position the later chapters even contradict the earlier ones; whereas if you think of them as having been written *before* chapters 1-9, the contradiction vanishes. Chapters 10-13 are a desperate (no other word for it) attempt by Paul to make the Corinthians accept him and his authority. Well, they had already done so according to chapters 9 and 10, and he had thanked God for it. Chapters 10-13 threaten the Corinthian church with severe action by way of discipline; in chapters 1-9 they have already taken action themselves, and there is nothing left for Paul but to be grateful for this, to commend them, and to concur in their judgment (2:5-11). The break between chapters 9 and 10 is not only one of subject matter or style; it is a violent change of mood, a change in situation. The efforts of some commentators to harmonize these chapters with the words and spirit of chapters 1-9 are most unconvincing.

Well, the main question is not when Paul wrote this but what he said and what it can mean for us. So let us get on with it.

Verses 1-6 of chapter 10 introduce the whole section (chs. 10-13) on the same note we hear again at the close: a warning to the disobedient. Paul uses strong language: "warfare . . . power to destroy . . . punish." This is not the mood nor the attitude of chapter 9. At the time he writes chapter 10 he is aware that not all is well at Corinth, that his authority is slipping. Just what the punishment is that he threatens, he does not say. Presumably it is excommunication. The one really obscure phrase here is "take every thought captive to obey Christ" (10:5). What this probably means is that he is not content with mere outward assent, or formal submission. "It is your very lives I want," he might have said. All through Paul's writings, or for that matter all through the Bible, the contrast is drawn between external and internal behavior. The severest condemnations of Jesus were for those Pharisees whose goodness was only in action that did not match the heart.

We should also take Paul at his best intention, not by what he sometimes sounds like. He is battling for his own authority, but he means it as a battle for the supremacy of Christ. It is not Paul the man but Paul as the representative of Christ who insists on obedience. This comes out in the next section also.

Boasting in the Lord (10:7-18)

Paul had enemies in Corinth at the time he wrote these lines, and we can guess what they must have said of him by his own replies. For one thing, apparently there were some who claimed a better right to be called "Christ's" than Paul had. It was not the last time in the long history of Christianity that individuals or groups have set themselves up as the only real Christians and tried to write off all the rest. Of the more than two hundred Protestant sects in the United States today, a great majority are very small, and will have nothing to do with one another, on the ground that only *we* have the truth. At Corinth it was apparently some of the local leaders, rather than a rival sect, who were causing Paul trouble.

Paul is about to indulge in some boasting, and he knows it; but he wants it understood that this was forced on him. A college professor with a Ph.D. or an Sc.D will ordinarily not write the letters after his name. But if someone has written to the dean accusing the professor of being a fake, and charging that his degrees were bought at a "diploma mill," then the mild-mannered professor may pay the dean an indignant visit, and insist on showing his genuine diplomas signed at distinguished universities. So when Paul has been attacked as an impostor, unless he is going to keep his mouth shut and apparently admit his guilt, he is bound to seem to boast.

One of the accusations against him was that his boldness increased with distance; that when faced with revolt he could roar like a lion if he were far enough away, but that when face to face with a church fight he only purred like a kitten. His enemies had even fallen to the level of making fun of his physical appearance. Tradition says that Paul was bowlegged, nearly bald, and short even by Mediterranean standards. Paul does not try to argue about his looks. What he says is that the Corinthians will find out, when he arrives, that his actions will be as bold as his letters. Paul will not compare himself with his critics; he wants to be taken on his own merits.

He reminds the Corinthians that he was the first to bring the gospel to them, which is more than his critics can claim. He hints that these critics have simply moved in after him and taken the credit for what Paul the pioneer had done. A bishop in India, speaking of the work of a certain sect, said that to his personal knowledge that sect had not won one single congregation from Hinduism. All its congregations had been started and built by telling the members of the older Christian churches that they were not really Christians till they joined the sect. It was this kind of thing that was distressful to Paul. (One entire letter of his, Galatians, was written largely about this matter.)

So Paul proceeds to "boast" in the Lord. What does this odd expression mean? It is part of a larger idea of Paul's, to *live in Christ;* that is, to live in constant relation to Christ, in union with him, in harmony with him, to keep Christ in one's thoughts at all times, to live as in his presence, to live as one does live, because of Christ. So to boast in the Lord means to boast when it is necessary—but only so far as is necessary; it means to boast in the light of Christ, to boast humbly, to boast only of one's achievements for Christ. Paul is well aware that while he has to speak of himself to keep the record straight and to refute the slanders being whispered against him, neither he nor any man can write his own recommendations. In more letters than one, but especially in Second Corinthians and Galatians, Paul highlights the fact, important to him and to us, that his authority came from God, not through men at all, and that the fact of this authority, the stamp of its genuineness, was the work he had so successfully done. The converts he had made (see ch. 3) were God's letter of recommendation of him; his enemies could show no such testimonials.

Paul's Right to Boast: His Sufferings in the Cause (11:1—12:10)

Paul now proceeds at some length, however, to exhibit more testimonials, and again of a kind that his critics could not duplicate.

First, he pays his disrespects to these men. The picture may come clearer if we think of them not as Corinthians, but as traveling preachers, self-styled apostles (remember the word "apostle" at that time was not confined to eleven men only). Paul's words are directed against them and also against such Corinthian Christians as were being taken in by these self-advertising gospel salesmen. (The situation is quite different from that pictured in chapters 1-9, where the whole letter is brightened by the news Paul has been told by Titus, that Paul's authority in Corinth was fully accepted and that the church had repented.)

These men are like the serpent when he seduced Eve (11:2-3). Following an Old Testament thought often occurring, but especially in Hosea, Paul thinks of religious faith as a kind of marriage. But whereas the Old Testament prophets thought of the husband as *God,* Paul speaks of betrothal to *Christ.* "I betrothed you to Christ" (11:2) may have reference to the Jewish custom of go-betweens or marriage brokers. Marriages were seldom decided on by the couple in question, but were arranged by the parents through professional marriage brokers.

The men who were undermining Paul's work at Corinth no doubt claimed to be Christian preachers, and no doubt preached "Christ." But Paul implies that the Christ they preached was not the real one, not the one *he* preached. Loyalty to Christ is a good phrase and a good thing—if the Christ to whom we are loyal is the real Christ. There were people at Corinth, and around us today, who although strongly loyal, cannot be called good Christians because their notions of Christ are so twisted. The false leaders at Corinth were seducing the Corinthians into loyalty to a "Christ" made in their own image.

Paul pours some sarcasm into the argument at this point. He comments on the ease with which the Corinthians fall for falsehood and distorted truths—for a different Jesus, for a different spirit (perhaps meaning a different Holy Spirit), for a different gospel. "I am not in the least inferior to these superlative apostles,"

Paul says. (It used to be thought that he meant the original Eleven, but now it is recognized that he uses the word "apostle" in the general sense of a traveling missionary, as was then common, and that he specifically means these impostors at Corinth. What he thought of real Apostles can be seen in I Corinthians 3.) He admits that he may not be the pulpit orator some of them are, but he has one advantage they do not have: he knows what he is talking about!

(It would be interesting if we had some copies of sermons preached by those visiting quacks. Maybe they never bothered to write anything; possibly they couldn't. But in any case the Corinthian church could stand them only about so long, and swept them out so completely that we don't even have their names, much less anything they said or wrote.)

Continuing in his ironic or sarcastic vein, Paul inquires what it was he had done that was so bad. Was it a sin that he preached without charging them any fees? (Apparently his rivals were in the ministry for revenue only.) Paul fairly shouts this "boast"; he will not be silent. *"When I . . . was in want, I did not burden any one."* He had taken from other churches but not from them.

Paul speaks in plain language about his competitors and would-be underminers; he undermines them in turn (vss. 12-15). They are false apostles, workmen who do not give an honest day's work, sheer hypocrites, clever as Satan at working up brilliant disguises. Paul turns again on the Corinthians with more sarcasm. They can't stand *him,* or some of them can't; but this is odd, for they seem to be able to stand a lot. These false apostles make slaves of them (they want to be dictators in ways that Paul would scorn to use); they prey on them (always after money); they put on airs; they actually use their fists on their church members. Alas, believe it or not, such "preachers" have existed in every Christian century. Paul speaks with still more sarcasm: "I am ashamed to say these are stronger men than I. I was too weak to play the part of wolf in the sheepfold!"

One of the most famous passages in this letter is 11:21—12: 10. Actually, Paul is neither bragging nor complaining. He is simply reporting some facts in his life, and doing this as a kind of challenge to those fake "apostles." The whole passage is part of his argument: I have the true marks of an Apostle: unselfish service, loyalty to the true Jesus, suffering in the service of Christ. What have these fly-by-night fakers to show, to match my record?

Paul does not appear to have arranged the items in his record for dramatic climax, he just pours them out as they occur to his mind. Whatever those others boast of, he can match, or go one better. He too is a Hebrew, an Israelite, a descendant of Abraham. To be sure, one can be no more an Israelite than another can. But as to being a servant of Christ, Paul can claim to be a better one. At this point he gives that amazing list of hardships, risks, and perilous adventures. He admits it sounds crazy to talk like this, but these are the facts. The reader may try, if he likes, to match verses 24-27 with the Book of Acts. Some of these incidents are recorded there, but most are not. These lines were written, of course, before Paul's voyage to Rome and the shipwreck described in Acts 27. But here we learn to our surprise that Paul had already been shipwrecked three times. (Maybe he never mentioned it to Luke; perhaps he never would have mentioned it if these false apostles hadn't pushed him into it.) No wonder he was a bit suspicious of setting out from Fair Havens so late in the fall! (Acts 27:9-10).

Since this letter was written well *before* the trip to Jerusalem recorded in Acts 20-21, it is clear that all the incidents mentioned in II Corinthians 11 and 12 must have occurred before that point in Paul's life. The fact that Acts mentions so few of them shows that the Book of Acts is not, and quite probably was not intended to be, a complete history of the period it covers.

In this impressive column of hardships and disasters, only two or three points need any word of comment. The "forty lashes less one" refers to an Old Testament law that no prisoner should be beaten with more than 40 strokes. As a safeguard, beatings were limited, in Paul's time, to 39 strokes. Since by custom the beating-strap was split into three thongs, only thirteen strokes were actually given. But even so, men had been known to die under the lash. The number of items here referring to travel hazards may remind us that travel was a dangerous undertaking. Mountains, canyons, and "breath-taking scenery" are quite different things when seen from the vista-dome of an air-conditioned fast train or a luxury jet-liner, and when seen by a traveler on foot, who has to ford or swim the rivers and who knows that every road of scenery may hide a gang of killers.

Again, in 12:1-10, Paul apologizes for the boasting he proceeds to do; though in verse 6 he says that properly speaking it is not boasting, but telling the simple truth. In most churches today "visions and revelations" of a direct sort are seldom claimed. Could you imagine a pulpit committee, when looking for a minister, selecting a man on the basis of the number and vividness of the visions he says he has had? But Paul was not in the twentieth century, he was in the first. At that time visions and revelations were not regarded with suspicion, but were believed to be marks of special saintliness as well as of authority. So he brings these in as further, and convincing, items in his self-defense.

All commentators agree that the "man" whom Paul knows can be only Paul himself. The vision he speaks of, but refuses to describe, is not mentioned in Acts, and we know nothing about it except from Paul's mysterious hints at this point. Questions come up: Are there really three heavens, or maybe more? Can a soul be caught up into heaven while the body still exists, living, here on earth? (Paul confesses he does not know.) Is Paradise the name for the third heaven only, or is it a name for any heaven or all of them? Paul uses the language of his time, and very likely the Corinthians understood him better than we can on this matter. The point is, he had had a vision, though he was not able to say what he had seen or heard. (He lays stress on what he heard, not on what he saw, which is typical of an intellectual man.) However, he is not going to claim special privileges on account of that experience. He does not wish to be pointed out as "the man who had the vision"! He wants to be taken for what he is, for what he now says and does. Again the practical side of Paul comes out.

In verse 7 he suggests that he had many such mystical experiences, and might have been conceited about them. We must remember that Paul grew up in an atmosphere that was not Christian, and that in those times it was a generally accepted belief that having many visions shows that a man is blessed of God, and many pains show that a man is under God's displeasure. So Paul had to discover for himself that the truth was something different. To keep him from being all "blown up" about the visions, God sent him severe pain, a "thorn . . . in the flesh."

Commentators ever since Paul's time have argued over what this thorn might be. You, the reader, know just as much about this as anybody else does. Maybe the Corinthians knew what Paul meant, maybe they did not. There are two separate uncertainties here. (a) Does this "thorn," or "stake," as many have translated it, refer to a mental-spiritual affliction or to physical pain? (b)

Does "flesh" mean what we would naturally take it to mean, the physical body, or does it mean man's nature as man, his humanity; or does it mean man's *sinful* nature? On question (a), we have no clue except that we usually interpret anyone literally if there is no reason to interpret otherwise. On question (b), we have to admit that Paul uses the word "flesh" in all three senses here mentioned (see, for example, Rom. 2:28 where the Greek has "flesh"; II Cor. 4:11; Gal. 5:16). Paul does not try to explain himself; but scholars have tried to do it for him. This expression has been understood to mean: *physical* pain, illness or deficiency of some kind (malaria? epilepsy? tuberculosis? weak eyes? glaucoma?); or something *mental-spiritual* (temptation in general? or temptation to some particular sin, perhaps pride or unchastity? or exposure to constant nagging, heckling, slander, and persecution?). Most Roman Catholic commentators incline to think this was temptation to impurity; most Protestant commentators are disposed to believe it was a physical ailment of a painful sort.

Whatever it was, Paul did not think it a good thing. He calls it a Devil's messenger. It must have been something that hampered him in his work as a missionary. Since everybody is entitled to one guess, your present commentator will venture one which at least is no worse than some others. What if this thorn in the flesh was not any one particular ailment or trouble of body or of mind? What if it was just that very common over-all ailment, an unattractive personality? Some personality defects are curable; some are not. When Paul compared himself with the steadiness of Peter, the smooth magnetic eloquence of Apollos; when he heard himself described as a man whose physical presence was weak, and whose sermon delivery was contemptible—might he not have wished to be made over into somebody with a more impressive front?

Well, whatever it was, this messenger of Satan also carried a message from God: "My grace is sufficient for you, for my power is made perfect in weakness." Paul would never have known this had he been the strong, self-sufficient person he longed and prayed to be. He learned through this hard experience, which may still have been going on at the time he wrote, that God sometimes refuses to give us what we want in order to give us what we need. He withholds gifts so we may desire *him*, without whom, as Augustine said, no gift can satisfy the soul.

This harsh experience of the Apostle has been a blessing to

the Church, too. Otherwise it could have been said: How could Christianity have missed? It was upheld and spread by a man of commanding powers, without a visible weakness, a man with no inner handicaps whatever. On the contrary, the most effective spokesman for Christ in the early years was this man Paul, a man who could be and was criticized and even despised by some, a man with real personal handicaps; yet a man filled with the Spirit. Paul spoke out of personal agony, personal discovery, when he wrote: "We have this treasure in earthen vessels" (II Cor. 4:7).

Paul Has Been More Than Fair (12:11-18)

Had Paul been writing an essay, 12:1-10 would have been a good climax. Nothing more needed to be said; nothing more profound could be said. Yet because this is a letter, not an essay, he goes on with a collection of anticlimaxes, as we all do in most of our letters. Once more, he says, he has been talking like a fool. He blames the Corinthians for it, because they have been swept off their feet by these "superlative apostles," the eccelesiastical impostors who have been blackening his name and motives. If they had eyes and memories, they should remember that "the signs of a true apostle" had been performed among them by Paul. What Paul means by this we do not know, unless it was the "signs and wonders and mighty works" (a stereotyped phrase for all kinds of miracles) of verse 12. The point is, what Paul had accomplished in Corinth marked him as a true Apostle, and they should have seen this. He points out, in sarcasm once more, that the poor Corinthians were mistreated in that Paul did not take any salary from them; he begs forgiveness for this mistreatment!

There is one more charge which Paul's enemies apparently brought against him: that his friends and representatives were crooked. This must have stung Paul sorely. He speaks sharply to defend Titus and "the brother" (unnamed here as in 8:18); they acted in the same generous and honest spirit shown by Paul.

Mend Your Ways, or Else—! (12:19-13:10)

After all, Paul says, it is not himself he has been defending; it is Christ, and it is for their sake rather than his own. Paul can see through the slanders of his critics; but some in Corinth cannot, and if they are misled their fate will not be good. Further, Paul feels that if the Corinthians follow these false apostles, they will drop right back into the quarreling, disorderly church they used to be; and the harmony not only among themselves but between themselves and Paul, themselves and God, will be broken.

Paul hangs his third visit over the Corinthians as a kind of threat. When the second visit was, no one knows; but 12:14 probably, and 13:1-2 certainly, show that there was a second visit not mentioned in Acts. It may have been very short.

Paul promises, in effect, not only to *have* the authority of an apostle, but to *use* it. He is not going to rush in blindly. Any charges (this is all vague as to details, but they no doubt knew what he meant) must be formally made and sustained by two or three witnesses. Nobody is going to be dealt with on mere suspicion.

But then Paul reminds these people, as he has before, that they themselves have all the right and power to deal with their local problems and problem-members. Examine *yourselves,* he says. Test *yourselves.* Even if they are spiritually stronger than he, and consequently better able than he to deal with their problems (a pretty wild supposition, to be sure), Paul will be glad of that. What I want and pray for, he says, "is your improvement."

Paul, by the way, is far from thinking that "what is to be is bound to be." He talks as a man can honestly talk only when he feels that men affect their "fate" by their own decisions. His language here (as well as elsewhere)—"I hope," "we pray," "unless indeed you fail to meet the test," "in order that when I come I may not have to be severe"—is not the language of a man who believes the future is already packaged and will finally be handed across time's counter just as it is wrapped up at this moment.

Farewell and Benediction (13:11-14)

Furthermore, Paul leaves off his letter writing with a constructive and not a critical thought. This may not be so much of an anticlimax, after all. After pointing out that his authority is for the purpose of building up, not tearing down, he closes with two benedictions, one with some "if's" attached, and then, after still other words of farewell, another benediction with no if's at all.

We said that this letter is a plea for harmony. This is certainly how Paul brings it to an end:

"Mend your ways" (your ways of discord and disorder);

"Heed my appeal" (for agreement with one another and with me);

"Live in peace" (not peace on Sunday only!);

". . . and the God of love and peace will be with you."

Not even an Apostle's benediction is automatic. Blessings cannot always be scattered like the rain, on the just and on the unjust. The blessings of God come, as Jesus had taught, to those who will receive them, not to those whose lives shut them out.

Like all Paul's letters, and like a musical symphony, this one seems to come to an end before it does. The real finale is, as Paul meant it to be, the great benediction of the last sentence. This is the only time Paul groups God the Father, Jesus Christ, and the Holy Spirit. Yet one may say that from this one "trinitarian" blessing comes a light to illumine the rest of the New Testament. If Paul never, or extremely seldom, says Jesus is God, here he does something even more remarkable; he mentions the Lord Jesus Christ first. For him, as for us, we do not understand Jesus by way of God; we come to God, we are laid hold of by God, we are reconciled to God, we know God, when we look into the face of Christ and receive through him the blessing of God Eternal. The God of Creation, speaking through the Law and the Prophets, and the Inmost God, the divine Spirit outpoured in the hearts of men, are one with the same Lord Jesus who for our sake was made to be sin, though he knew no sin—the same Lord Jesus in whose face shines the glory of God.